Money and How to Make More of It

Money and How to Make More of It

Lorraine Chase and Adam Shaw

CASSELL PLC

ORION BUSINESS
BOOKS

Dedicated to the memory of John Knight who was the inspiration for this book and much more.
L.C.

To my mum and dad – Rita and Tommy – who showed me the meaning of value.
A.S.

First published in Great Britain in 1998 by
Orion Business
An imprint of The Orion Publishing Group Ltd
Orion House, 5 Upper St Martin's Lane, London WC2H 9EA

A CIP catalogue record for this book
is available from the British Library.

ISBN 0-75281-223 8

Designed and typeset by Blackjacks
Printed in Great Britain by Butler & Tanner Ltd, Frome and London

Contents

INTRODUCTION
from Lorraine Chase

I know what you're thinking – the name Chase is 'ardly synonymous with the City! What 'ave finances and Lorraine Chase got in common? You'd be right. Nothing, absolutely nothing! A fact I wanted to change. Why? I'll tell you. Until recently I'd been too busy to worry about my finances. And before I was too busy to worry about my finances, I didn't 'ave any finances worth worrying about. So I suppose you could say that a culmination of circumstances has brought about this moment in time.

By trying to change my financial know-how (sorry, my lack of it) I realised there was a large hole in the financial book market. Oh sure, there were books for the beginner, those with a splattering of knowledge, those who'd always 'ad a little interest and wanted to learn more. Not, 'owever, a book for the absolute beginner, a virgin to the financial world. Sadly, as in all things, life is made very difficult when you're 'andicapped with a bad education. Every interest you take up, every opportunity offered is made into an obstacle and a chore, because of a lack of the most basic knowledge. Who knows, with a little sprinkling of Latin, my interest in flowers and my association with plant life might have bloomed even further!

My quest for knowledge started with a hop and a skip to Dillons. "Excuse me, but could you suggest a book on finance for the absolute beginner please?" I asked sheepishly. "The financial section is over there," waved the bloke behind the counter. Sounded promising I thought. He's obviously confident I'll find what I want, and his assistance is unnecessary!

Oh dear. Two hours later and I'd got, at best, an 'opeful. It turned out to be for the American market. I 've no excuses, but my mind must've been addled by all those millions of confusing books. But as in all things, life can be changed by a twist of fate.

I later bumped into Adam Shaw at a Champagne tasting at the Dorchester.

"Don't I know you?" I asked. " 'Ang on, don't tell me. It'll come to me, give me a minute.... er... gotcha! You're Adam Shaw from the box. You're on Working Lunch and Business Breakfast! I've bin putting you on the telly while I do 20 minutes on me semi-recumbent." (cycling machine to you). The poor man then got a diatribe re. My Efforts To Gain Business Acumen. Yet 'is patience and 'onest interest astounded me. What a nice geezer, I thought.

"I think someone ought to write a book to 'elp people like me,"
I suggested. "The trouble is 'cos the authors know the subject they're writing about they forget 'ow confusing it is for the likes of me, and the reader doesn't get past first base. We need to make our money work these days, every penny counts. Jobs are no longer for life!"

Adam agreed, and an idea was born. Eureka!

We 'ope this books is arranged in such a way that the reader can pick it up, read a page or two and put it down. Use the book for reference as well as to amuse.

This book can be left on a coffee table and (we 'ope) even the younger members of the family might pick it up, look at the cartoons and maybe – just maybe – become interested enough to 'ave a read. Wouldn't it be grand if some future City big wig confessed his interest for City wheeling and dealing flourished because 'e flipped through a copy of 'Money and How To Make More Of It' on 'is mother's coffee table?

INTRODUCTION
from Adam Shaw

For too long, too many people have felt that finance was a club they didn't have the right to join. As a result the world of stocks and shares, bonds and bears, has remained elitist. It has developed the mythical trappings of all such clubs, with its secret language, snobbishness and exclusion of the uninitiated.

But the fast lives of the wheelers and dealers are to a great extent funded by the very people who feel most excluded. It's the money which we all put into our pension funds which form some of the biggest investments in the financial markets. The irony is therefore, that we are already steeped in this world of finance, even if we have been unaware of it.

In this book we don't want to persuade you to invest more, we do want to help empower anyone with savings, so they can understand and control the forces which make their money grow. This book is not just about money, PEPS and derivatives – it's about £15.99 and cheap at half the price and we hope that will be one of the better investments you will make.

This is no whizz kid guide to fame and fortune, but it is a place to start learning the basics and a little beyond – a book in which you can find out about bulls, bears, rabbits and why you must feed the goldfish.

As Mary Quant said: "Having money is rather like being a blonde. It is more fun but not vital." Of course without savings, it is very difficult to think about investments, but you don't need much spare cash to benefit from a clear investment strategy. Even a little dabble in the markets can be fun and exciting and provide you with an opportunity for a bit of profit

There's no harm in taking advice and you don't need to know all the answers or even all the questions, before you start looking at the investment world and trying to take care of your savings. Even if you don't want to make a fortune, you still have to work just to protect the value of your savings and to do that, you will need to understand the language of finance and the choices which are available.

Remember there are risks in all investments and money can always be lost as well as gained. Certainly this book may not make you rich, but hopefully it will help you look after your money in a way that suits you best. And if you do want to get into the financial fast lane, it will at least provide you with a map so you know where you are going

A. Shaw

CHAPTER 1
Money And How To Make More Of It

Funny 'ow things we come across as children come back to haunt us through life. It seems to me that things don't change. People often want to exclude you from one thing or another by the art of language. To make more of what they know, they tell you very little or they make things more complicated than they really are. Academics, industry and (yes!) the City are all guilty to different degrees.

When I was a kid, my Skin and Blister (oops, sorry, my sister) three years my senior, 'ad a way of talking to 'er friends, a language that only a chosen few could understand. It was called Butcher Talk. To be 'onest I was never sure 'ow she did it (which of course was the whole idea) but it was somehow done by adding certain letters to the beginning and end of words. It was 'er way of excluding non-members of the gang, of ostracising outsiders and making them feel insecure, small and not worthy. She wasn't a nasty sister, she was just protecting 'erself and 'er adolescent secrets from little ol' me, who might tell Mum and Dad at anytime and get 'er into trouble.

Bears, Bulls and Stags are just a few bits of City jargon designed to keep you guessing. And why not? Advisers earn their money from commission or annual charges. He or she gets dosh every time they do a transaction. If the deal does well, you make a few quid and they get their commission. If the deal goes badly, you lose a few quid and they <u>still</u> get their commission. Nice work if you can get it, eh? No wonder they like to keep people dependent on advisers.

But in reality, investing is no Black Magic. <u>I've</u> learnt 'ow to do it, which means more or less anyone can. So me and my mate Adam 'ave fought through all the difficult bits and laid out an easy step by step guide on 'ow to play the markets, buy and sell, invest for the long term and 'opefully make lots of dosh while 'aving a bit of fun at the same time.

> Who is Tessa?
>
> How risky is it?
>
> Can I get rich?
>
> How do I get advice?

These are just a few of the questions I started with, and if this is what's been bothering you, glance through this book and you'll find the answers you want, and more besides. Of course it's not just about learning stuff you didn't know before. What we're going to show you is that finance isn't as complex as it's cracked up to be. Give yourself a little time, turn a few of these pages and you'll find you won't 'ave to blindly trust others for advice. While it probably won't turn you into a millionaire, this book should give you confidence enough to 'elp turn your pennies into pounds and understand 'ow best to use your savings. But before we go any further, 'ere's Adam's own 'Guru Guide' to investment rules.

A GURU'S GUIDE

Adam Shaw's Guru Guide to Investment

The only things we know are that maths is hard, politicians lie and toast falls butter side down. There are no other certainties in life, least of all that investments will make a fortune or even keep up with inflation. However there is no sadder thing than the musty smell of mouldy tenners and so once you have a little bit of savings, it's a crime not to do something with your hard earned, unspent money. The question is just what to do?

Beware of the rabbits. They're fun, fluffy and altogether fabulous, but they get transfixed by headlights and run over. Interest rates, yields, P/E ratios and dividends can also blind the would-be investor. Unless you know what they mean and how important they are, it's easy to be disoriented and transfixed by the jargon. It's appealing to think that if you don't do anything, you can't make a mistake. But

that's not true – just standing there means you're likely to get run over. Money in your current account is losing value every day, even with the small amount of interest that you earn, so you'll still be able to buy less with it next year than you can today. Being a bunny is not an option. You have to do something that helps you beat inflation – and gives you a chance to do even better than that.

There are six types of basic investments: bank/building society accounts, shares, bonds, derivatives, currency holdings, and commodities. Amongst that lot, there is a choice for everyone, from those who set three alarm clocks every morning and look both ways when crossing the road, to the leather-clad biking speed-merchant who thinks of nothing but the next dare-devil bend in the road.

The Great Divide is not the Rift Valley in Africa, the sea trench under the ocean or the rivalry between Glasgow Rangers and Celtic. The one character-forming, earth shattering, self-realising revelation is the moment when you discover whether you are a speculator or an investor. There may be no football shirts or terrace chants, but take a train full of commuters and beneath the suits and behind the pages of the daily rag, beat the hearts of two very different tribes. The investor wants to know there's a very decent chance of coming out on top. Their steady and methodical heart-beats can't take the wild swings of massive profit and mortgage-threatening loss. The speculator on the other hand needs that shot of adrenalin and while they hate their losses, the prospect of enormous gain makes the gamble worth the risk.

Banks, building societies and government bonds are all relatively safe, or at least predictable, investments. Shares – and to a greater extend, derivatives, currencies and commodities – represent a leap into the unknown. You can gain everything and lose everything. In the funfair that is the investment market this is the roller coaster, not the merry go round.

You've got to feed the goldfish. It's no good just buying your fish, chucking it in the tank and then forgetting about it. Fish need to be fed, the water needs to be changed and at Christmas they need to be bought an under-water arch to swim through. Neglect them and one morning you wake up to find them floating at the top of the tank. Investments, speculative or otherwise, are much the same. It's no good putting your money in shares, bank accounts or bonds and forgetting about them. Money has to be looked after. Neglect it, and it will neglect you.

Don't talk to strangers. There'll be plenty of people willing to advise you on exactly where you should put your hard earnt money. The people who are offering advice are also usually trying to sell you something. The financial market place is like any other market and it's best to go to someone you know or trust, not just the latest person to knock on your door or telephone you. The more informed you are about the products on offer and the clearer you are about what you want from an investment, the more likely you are to profit from the deal. Make sure you come away with an outfit that fits, not an oversized nylon shirt in last year's lime green stripes that no one else will buy.

To him that hath, shall be given. Unfortunately the world of riches is not a democracy. If you have money, it's easier to make more of it. But having a little extra cash is not the only thing you need to turn your pennies into pounds. It's easier to make a fortune if you know what you're doing. And while you won't find any cash lurking between the pages of this book, you will find plenty of information which will help you make the right decisions on how to put your savings to best use.

There are millions of people in Britain who own shares, and many of them are just ordinary people who have decided to give it a go with relatively small amounts of money. One of the things which attracted many of these people to the stockmarket is that in the past, share investments have performed very well and made investors much more money than they could have done had they let their savings lie in a bank or building society.

For instance, one thousand pounds invested in a building society in 1973 would, twenty years later, be worth just under six thousand pounds. But the same thousand pounds invested in shares which reflected the performance of the stockmarket as a whole, would have performed twice as well as that – they would be worth nearly twelve thousand pounds.

In fact if you take account of inflation and look over an even longer term, investing in the stockmarket looks much more appealing. Since the end of the Second World War, money left in a building society would have halved in value – meaning that after inflation has eaten away at it, you could now only buy half the things you could fifty years ago. However if you took the money you put in your building society and invested it on the stockmarket and re-invested all your dividends and gains, you would now be able to buy ten times the amount of things you could fifty years ago.

Lorraines's Little Somethings

I was asking a friend at Barclays Stockbrokers to work out what exactly would have happened to your dosh had you put it in a building society, bought equities or shoved it under the mattress. This is what he said:

BUILDING SOCIETY: *£100 invested in 1945 with interest reinvested would be worth £1,063 in 1996*

EQUITIES: *£100 invested in 1945 would be worth £25,017 in 1996*

BED: *£100 in under your bed would be worth £2,500 to a money collector, just for its historic value. In addition to that, you'd 'ave 'ad the use of the mattress for the last 50 years.*

Well who'd 'ave thought !

Looked at in this way it does appear that the stockmarket can make you lots of money – but only if you pick the right shares. Unlike a building society or bank, the stockmarket can also be a risky place. Although you can make lots of money, you can lose lots as well.

While there are millions of shareholders, many of them own just one or two shares. They bought into British Gas or one of the other privatisations but haven't ventured any further into the stockmarket. Part of the reason for this is that many people don't feel comfortable dealing with bankers, brokers or financial advisers and would never dream of turning to the strange pink pages of the *Financial Times*. But investing is not as difficult as it may first seem.

In fact choosing an investment is a bit like baking a cake: you never really know what's going to happen until the cake has come out of the oven. The secret of success lies in making sure you've got the right ingredients, knowing just how to mix them together and ensuring your timing is right so the cake is baked and not burnt.

WHICH INVESTMENT?

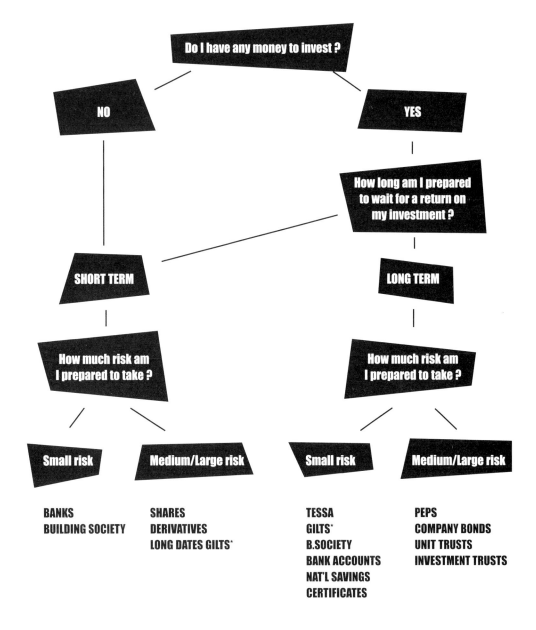

Do I have any money to invest ?

NO

YES

How long am I prepared to wait for a return on my investment ?

SHORT TERM

LONG TERM

How much risk am I prepared to take ?

How much risk am I prepared to take ?

Small risk

Medium/Large risk

Small risk

Medium/Large risk

BANKS	SHARES	TESSA	PEPS
BUILDING SOCIETY	DERIVATIVES	GILTS*	COMPANY BONDS
	LONG DATES GILTS*	B.SOCIETY	UNIT TRUSTS
		BANK ACCOUNTS	INVESTMENT TRUSTS
		NAT'L SAVINGS	
		CERTIFICATES	

* *PLEASE NOTE: GILTS offer a guaranteed rate of interest and the face value of the gilt is fully repayable when it matures. In the long run therefore the investor knows precisely what will happen to their investment, as long as it is held until the gilt has matured. It is therefore thought of as a relatively safe, or at least predictable, investment. However, those looking for short term gains by buying gilts which still have a long time to run before they mature are gambling on short term movements in the tradable price of the gilt. Gilt prices can be volatile and therefore gilt investments used as part of a short term strategy are medium to high risk investments.*

JUSTIN'S JIGSAW

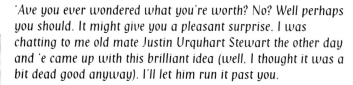

'Ave you ever wondered what you're worth? No? Well perhaps you should. It might give you a pleasant surprise. I was chatting to me old mate Justin Urquhart Stewart the other day and 'e came up with this brilliant idea (well, I thought it was a bit dead good anyway). I'll let him run it past you.

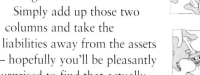

To most of us, our financial affairs bear more resemblance to the dusty and rather decrepit looking family jigsaw box which contains hundreds of different pieces. Very rarely have we sat down to actually complete the jigsaw and there has always been a sneaking concern that in fact some of the pieces, probably the vital ones, are missing.

Putting together our jigsaw of personal financial affairs is a lot easier than you might think. Also, once you've done it, it's easy to update and make sure that any missing pieces are replaced and any damage is repaired.

So how do we actually go about assembling the jigsaw? Very simply, I believe the best thing to do is to complete a personal balance sheet. This is a list of your assets – the things you own – and you liabilities – the things you owe.

Firstly your assets. Write down list of the things you own: an indication of the value of your house or flat, the value of your car, or in my case motorcycle. Add your pension and life assurance policies. You may have a bit of a problem with the last two as the statements are not always that clear – but you can phone up the company who sold them to you and ask what they are worth.

Don't forget your other savings and investments like shares, bonds, unit and investment trusts, national savings and grandma's premium bonds. I also like to include a rough indication of the value of the major household goods and valuables. It's not a precise science, but it does give you an indication of your assets.

With regard to your liabilities, this tends to be easier. Unfortunately, those we owe money to remind us of it on a fairly regular basis. This list should include the amount we owe on our mortgage, any overdraft or bank loans as well as credit cards, store cards and any other items we have bought on credit.

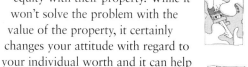

Simply add up those two columns and take the liabilities away from the assets – hopefully you'll be pleasantly surprised to find that actually your net worth is considerably higher than you originally thought. This is particularly encouraging for those who are either in, or are close to, negative equity with their property. While it won't solve the problem with the value of the property, it certainly changes your attitude with regard to your individual worth and it can help in your discussions with the mortgage provider.

There are, however, two other elements which I believe are important to the family jigsaw. Firstly it's important to update it – every six months is, in my view, about right. This enables you to track what your net worth is and hopefully how it is growing. And it also keeps you on track for any longterm plans. The second issue is that we should try and include families or partners where appropriate in our calculations of assets and liabilities.

Like any good jigsaw, once the pieces are in place, the picture of your financial world suddenly becomes far clearer. It is then particularly helpful in showing up areas that may be missing or look a little raggedy round the edges.

By nature we tend to deal with one financial issue and problem at a time. We rarely link them all together and see how they interact with each other. The jigsaw helps us to be able to do that and prevents us from not only missing certain issues but also encourages us to take action when we find pieces are missing.

So dust down the old jigsaw box, reassemble your pieces and find out how much you are worth!

BALANCE SHEET

ASSETS

PROPERTY:
House/Flat/Other

PENSION:

ASSURANCE/
ENDOWMENT POLICY

SAVINGS:
Bank/B.Society/TESSA/OTHER

VALUABLES:

INVESTMENTS:
PEP/Share/Gilts/Bonds/Other

OTHERS
(Not previously mentioned)

TOTAL (A)..

LIABILITIES

MORTGAGE

BANK LOAN:

HIRE PURCHASE:

CREDIT CARDS:

STORE CARDS:

CAR LOANS:

OTHERS
(Not previously mentioned)

TOTAL (B)..

A-B = NET WORTH £...

PANTOMIME FINANCE

One of my favourite traditional scenes in pantomime 'as always been the 50p gag. There are several of these little scenes that re-occur each year, all under different names (the slosh scene, the busy bee or the magic 'at routine). They're all great fun and very traditional. The gags are the same whatever the storyline and whatever the characters. This one's from Cinderella and 'ere's 'ow it goes.

The scene is between Buttons, Baron Hardup, the Dame and the Conductor of the orchestra.

BARON HARDUP: "Buttons, I'm so glad I caught you. Where's that pound you owe me."

BUTTONS: "I'm sorry Baron Hardup, I'm strapped for cash at the moment, but I'll get it from someone else. Excuse me Mr Conductor Sir, but could I borrow £1 please."

CONDUCTOR: "Sorry Buttons, but I'm afraid I haven't got £1, but I could lend you 50p."

BUTTONS: "Thank you. There you are Baron, I haven't got £1 but I can give you 50p and I'll owe you 50p."

BARON HARDUP: "Thank you Buttons."

THE DAME ENTERS STAGE LEFT AND SEEING BARON HARDUP, WALKS OVER TO HIM

DAME: "Ah, you are Baron, I was hoping I'd find you here. I've come to collect that pound you owe me.

BARON: "I'm so sorry Dame, but I haven't got the pound, but I can give you 50p and owe you 50p"

BUTTONS: "Talking of owing money, Dame you owe me £1."

DAME: "Why that's right, I'm terrible sorry, I don't have £1 but I do have 50p, I'll give you that and owe you 50p."

BUTTONS: "Thank you. There you are Baron there's the 50p I owe you. Now we're all square."

BARON: "Thank you Buttons. There you are Dame, there's the 50p I owe you. Now we're all square."

DAME: "Thank you Baron. There you are Buttons, there's the 50p I owe you. Now we're all square."

BUTTONS: "Thank you Dame. There you are Mr Conductor, there's the 50p I owe you. Now we're all square."

You're probably all confused, but do read it again. I think it's quite brilliant and a fair description of my finances.

CHAPTER 2

Stock Pickers

YOUR GUIDE TO SHARES, THE STOCKMARKET AND HOW TO PROFIT FROM THEM

"OK POP Pickers, That was the Big Blue. Next up are the men in white coats with their latest single, 'Eye See Eye'

One of the biggest explosions in share ownership is happening right now, as building societies give up their mutual status and turn themselves into banks. Millions of building society members are being handed free shares in the new banks – effectively doubling the size of the share owning public. Many of them will be tempted to sell their shares, then either bank the profits or go out and spend it on a slap-up meal for two. But there's lots of reasons why they should do neither.

Well they'd better be good reasons 'cos a romantic champagne dinner for two sounds good to me.

Sounds good to me too, but the fun you get from a good share lasts a lot longer than the bubbles in a glass of champagne. And although share investments offer no guarantees, the fact is that on average, a stockmarket investment has regularly provided returns much higher than the rate of inflation and most other types of investments as well.

Alright then, how much dosh are we talking 'ere? I think most of us assume that investments are not an option unless you've got a lot of money.

Well you don't need to be rich to invest, but it does make sense to have a little money to play with before you start buying shares. When you buy or sell shares there is a minimum fee which the broker charges for trading on your behalf. It's hardly worth it therefore to buy just one share. If you've got a hundred pounds or more to play with, then I think it starts to make sense.

And Adam, if you don't have much money I've heard there's always the opportunity of sorting out an investment club. Tell you more about that later.

There are two basic ways of investing in the stockmarket. Unit trusts and investment trusts provide a way to invest in shares without having to pick the specific companies you think will do well. The trust managers take your money and invest it in a wide range of shares. This method offers you a spread of investments you may not have otherwise been able to get with only a limited amount of money to invest. On the other hand, if you want to be a bit more adventurous, you can pick your own shares in the hope that you can choose a soaraway success.

CHOOSING SHARES THE PICK AND MIX WAY

"Two pounds of ICI, a quarter of MOS, a bucketful of Guinness and a packet of Rolos, please."

Of course even if the stockmarket has in the past provided a very attractive means of making money, it doesn't mean every share has offered great returns. Even when the stockmarket is soaring, it's still possible to pick shares which are heading in the opposite direction. So the secret of benefiting from the rise in general share prices is to make sure you pick the right shares. The ideal is to buy a share when it's dirt cheap and sell when it's disgustingly expensive, then run down the road screaming and yelling for joy with a fat wad of fivers. Of course, that's easier said than done, but while there is no guaranteed path to success, there are plenty of pointers which may help you on your way.

There are two ways of making money from shares.

1 Firstly, because shareholders are part owners of the company in which they have invested, they are entitled to a share of the profit the company makes. Normally companies divide a portion of their profit amongst the shareholders, in proportion to the amount of shares they own. The more shares you have, the larger the proportion of the profit you will be entitled to. Normally these profits are distributed twice a year. The distribution is called a dividend, paid as an interim dividend and a final dividend.

If the company gets into trouble or has a change of policy, the dividend payments can be suspended, so that shareholders receive no payout – very nice for the postman who has a lighter sack, but not so great for the shareholders.

Lorraines's Little Somethings

Recently I 'eard about a six year old chimpanzee that beat Sweden's top stockmarket analysts in choosing the best performing shares. The chimp picked the share by throwing darts at a board, whilst the others sweated over corporate reports. The monkey had more fun and made more money at the end of it. I wonder whether Swedish investors are particularly dumb, Swedish chimps are particularly bright or if it just goes to show that all the high talk of stockmarket analysis ain't as good as a bloomin' good hunch.

2 The second path to making money is the hope that your shares will increase in value and you can therefore sell them at a profit. That profit is dependent on what happens to the price of your shares, which is determined by many things, not all of them strictly intelligent or predictable.

The prospects for the company's business is reflected in the price of the share. So a company which seems to be doing very well, deserves to be valued highly. Share prices are also affected by the demand and supply of the shares on the stockmarket. So if a lot of people decide to sell their shares and not many people want to buy them, the price will fall to a level at which the buyers are persuaded to come into the market and pick up a bargain.

Perhaps more unfairly, a share price can also be affected by issues outside the control of the company's management. Changes in interest rates, political uncertainty and rumours can all have a major influence on the price of shares. That may not be fair, but whoever said life was fair? If you have a penchant for purchasing shares, two ways of judging a good buy are the P/E ratio and the dividend yield.

What is a P/E ratio?

Well the P/E, or price earning ratio, tells you how many times you have to multiply the company's profits to equal the value of all its shares.

But exactly how does knowing this help your investment decisions? A company which is expected to grow very quickly and increase its profits in the future might have a high P/E ratio. Investors have high expectations for this company and by purchasing the shares you are gambling that the company will do as well as expected. But if it fails to meet those high expectations, the share price is likely to fall. Therefore be wary of companies with very high P/E ratios.

Conversely a company whose shares have a low P/E ratio, may be expected to grow slowly in the future. Investors have low expectations for its future growth. You are still gambling that the company will do as well as expected, it's just that the expectations aren't so great. It is less likely to fail. Therefore companies with low P/E ratios tend to be less risky.

In early 1997 Marks and Spencer shares had a P/E ratio of 18 and World of Leather had a P/E ratio of 30. That doesn't mean World of Leather is twice as good a company as M&S but it does mean investors think there is more room for improvement at World of Leather.

Now as a guide to finding companies which are growing, P/E ratios are by themselves only rough and ready reckoners. To begin with, they look at past performance and not future performance, and looking back is not always the best way of judging what's in front of you.

THE P/E SCHOOL OF MOTORING

The P/E ratios quoted in the newspapers are historic. Which means that they are based on the company's past performance. But you can also work out the prospective P/E ratio, which rather than looking back, looks ahead. Prospective P/E ratios are based on predictions of a company's profits given either by the company itself or by analysts. You can find details of these predictions in occasional reports in the press and media. Of course this bit of crystal ball gazing is not always accurate, so profit predictions should come with a warning.

But if you fancy a quick trip back to the maths class, here's how to work a P/E ratio out.

Profits After Tax ÷ Number of shares = Earnings per share

Share Price ÷ Earnings per share = P/E ratio

Although they are helpful in understanding shares, there are a few words of warning about using the P/E ratio, which are worth hearing (see left).

The other big thing to watch out for is the dividend. The dividend is the payment the companies make to their shareholders. If everything is going well, you can expect one to land on your doormat twice a year, which can give your cash flow a bit of a boost. In addition to the dividend income you may get, what you hope is that the share price increases, so you can sell it at a profit.

WARNING

Don't make an investment decision based entirely on the P/E ratio, it's only part of the way to judge the value of a share. P/E ratios should only be used to compare companies within the same sector, so it's a good way of comparing BP and Shell, but not a good way of comparing ICI and Marks and Spencer. P/E ratios are not good ways of comparing companies in different countries.

A share should therefore not be chosen purely for the size of the expected dividend payout. While dividend payments are very welcome, by themselves they rarely match the return you could get by putting your money in other safer investments.

If you want to compare the dividends paid by different companies, you need to look at the dividend yield. But dividend yields also help you compare the performance of shares with other types of investments, such as bank deposit accounts.

Just like the P/E ratio, dividend yields are historic and tell you what has happened in the past, not what will happen in the future. Many companies suspend dividend payments if they find themselves in financial trouble or have a change of heart about just how much of their profits should be distributed amongst shareholders. If a company decides not to pay a dividend one year, ordinary shareholders miss out on that forever and cannot claim the money back when the company is performing better.

INVESTMENT TIP
THE ASSET NET

If a company looks like it might go bust, the net asset value is likely to provide an indication of the base below which the value of the shares will not fall. But do not use this as your only guide. Net asset value is an assessment of the company's worth, and when it comes to selling all the company's bits and pieces they may not fetch as much as was expected. The net asset value also does not take into account the tax which must be paid out of the proceeds from any asset sale.

So let's get to what the dividend yield exactly does. In short, it tells you how much bang you get for your buck – or in other words how much income you'll get for every pound or penny you spend on the share. The dividend yield is calculated by:

Gross Dividend Per Share
÷ Share Price x 100   = Divided Yield measured as a percentage

For instance, *Chase Me* shares cost 100 pence and the dividend was 10 pence. The dividend yield is therefore 10% (10÷100x100 = 10%). If the share price collapses to 50 pence the dividend yield is still based on last year's dividend payout, which was 10 pence. But now the 10 pence dividend is a larger proportion of the share price. The dividend yield is 20%. (10÷50x100 = 20%). The dividend yield has risen but only because investors have lost confidence in the company and depressed its share price. It does not mean there will be a larger dividend cheque coming through the post.

Worth mentioning (but rarely the most important indicator of a share's value as an investment) is the net asset value, otherwise

WARNING
Be careful if you see a company with an unusually high dividend yield. Ironically the yield may have been pushed higher because the price of the shares have fallen. Large falls in the price of a share may mean the company is in trouble and future dividends may be suspended.

known as NAV. This is the total value of a company if it were broken up and sold in pieces, and is calculated by assessing the value of its assets and deducting the value of its liabilities.

In fact a company's shares are usually worth much more than the net asset value, which at first may strike you as odd. This is because investors are usually interested not just in the break up value of the company, but its future potential for profits. For some companies however, the net asset value is a much more important measure of the shares' worth, such as property companies or investment trusts, where the value of the assets are the basis of the company's profits.

Although there are quite a few other measures of a company's health which we haven't mentioned, using the little measuring tools here should give you a fair start in the game of judging which shares will do best.

ADAM'S INVESTMENT TIP
BUYING ON A DIP

The stockmarket has historically performed very well. Even after major setbacks it doesn't seem to take too long to get back on its feet. So if you have the courage, the idea is to buy shares when the market collapses. Watch for a 10% fall in the FTSE Index – there was one in 1987, 1990 and 1992 – and then buy some blue chip shares.

The market fell 400 points between mid-July and mid-September 1990, a fall of just over 16%. Within a year it had risen by 30% from the low point and was about 8% higher than the level from which the crash started.

British Airways shares were trading at about 580p in July 1990, by mid-September they had fallen to around 400p, a fall of 31%. Within a year it had risen by 70% from its low and was 17% higher than the level from which it fell.

Of course buying shares as the market collapses can be a very high risk strategy and there is no guarantee that history will repeat itself and you'll make money from buying at the cheap end.

Now Adam, what do you know about these penny shares? I just love the name. They sound very solid and cosy (not to mention cheap and cheerful). To be honest I think the name reminds me of those dear little Georgian Prints I used to collect: "a penny plain and tuppence coloured". Do you know the ones I mean? I mentioned my interest in these shares to a colleague of mine who warned me to stay clear, so give us the lowdown. Are they a risky investment, or as sweet as the name suggests?

Well the share price may be low, but there's a reason for that, and it's because the company has been in a whole load of trouble or people think it's very risky. You can buy as few penny shares as you like, but with the broker's commission an average £20, it makes little sense to buy in small quantities.

Of course if the company picks up, you can make a big profit because you have bought in so cheap. Also, you can cross your fingers and hope that someone buys the company to take advantage of its stockmarket quotation, in which case the price of the shares might go up.

So, at the end of the day, penny shares can be a good investment, but they are a risky way of getting into the stockmarket.

CHASE'S CHOCOLATE CHEESECAKE

4oz Sweetmeal biscuits	250g Marscapone cheese
2 handfuls of chopped nuts	1½ oz caster sugar
1oz butter	Bar of chocolate to make
3½ oz chocolate	decorations

First crush yourself some of your favourite sweetmeal biscuits. 4oz of them to be exact. Then mix some chopped nuts and about 1oz of melted butter.

Sort yourself out a 7" cake tin and viciously splat the mixture into it. Press and push the mixture down, until it lines the tin. Oh, and before you do any of that stuff, I should 'ave asked you to put the oven on at 150°C and get it up to speed so that you can now shove your biscuit lined cake tin in for 20 minutes. After 20 minutes, yank it out and let it cool. Turn the oven up to 200°C, which is the temperature we'll need to cook at.

Now 'ere's where the fun begins. For all you fellow chocoholics, this could be heaven, or this could be hell. Melt 3.5oz of chocolate in a bain marie. Don't know what that means? Neither did I 'til I looked it up. It's a pan of boiling water with a Pyrex bowl over it. Put the would-be melted chocolate into the bowl. Keep stirring the chocolate and once it's started to melt, turn the heat down so the water isn't boiling furiously.

At this point the smell of said melting chocolate drives any self respecting chocoholic mad, so don't fight it, shove a nice clean finger in and 'ave a good suck. NO!!!! Don't you dare put it in second time ... oh alright, but wash it first. Is that fab or is that fab??? Less of the frivolity now, onwards and upwards.

Mix 250g of Marscapone cheese with 1.5oz of caster sugar. Do what? Of course this isn't fattening. Add the melted chocolate to the mixture and toss the lot into your baking tin. Put it back into the oven and bake for 90 minutes.

I tell you, this stuff is to die for. If you want to be really wicked, chuck chocolate whirls all over it. You can make the whirls by dragging a carrot grater over a hard bar of chocolate.

And there you have it – Enjoy!!!

SHAW'S SUCCESSFUL SHARES

Choosing a share which won't sink, is a little more difficult than baking a cake which won't sink - but in many ways the skills are similar: in both cases you must start with good ingredients, timing is important and you need a little luck to make sure your cake has risen and not collapsed.

When baking cakes, make sure you have top quality chocolate and cheese. When choosing shares, make sure you have top quality income potential and capital growth.

Of course it's much easier finding a good bar of chocolate than finding a top share performer. Finding a company which you think will give you both income and capital growth is the equivalent of stumbling across a double choc, fruit and nut mega bar.

Dividends provide income, usually twice a year. Fast growing companies provide you with the profit you hope to make by selling your shares for more than you bought them.

INVESTMENT CLUBS

Why not create your own investment club? If you and a few of your mates or family are of a like mind, and are interested in the possibility of investing, why not go for it? That way you can enjoy an evening on a regular basis where you can discuss your thoughts and ideas. You should all put an affordable monthly sum into a kitty and when you've got enough to invest, you're on your way.

I don't know about you, but I find this idea of an investment club appealing. It makes it more fun, and turns it into an interesting and social hobby rather than an isolated preoccupation. It expands your knowledge with the other members' input and ideas, and when the pot is large enough you can share the thrill of the chase.

Come on ladies! Grab the male-dominated investment world by the scruff of the neck and give it bleedin' good shake. Form a crèche for the kids and 'old the meetings in each others' flats or 'ouses. Take time to learn a new experience together. A girl friend of mine got together with other ladies when she was carrying 'er son. The ladies (all in similar condition) met up once or twice a week and very successful they were at it too. She bought 'er 'ouse with the proceeds!

There are lots of books on this subject. "Investment Clubs" by Tony Dury is a good example. It's easy to read, very informative, and includes 'visits' to five clubs where you can sample the benefits of this idea, as well as offering details on 'ow to set one up and conduct your meetings. Most of the clubs in Britain belong to ProShare the organisation which aims to promote wider share ownership. The ProShare Investment Club manual tells you everything you need to know about setting up and running a club. Contact ProShare for details on 0171 394 5200

In America, investment clubs are more popular (53% of the US stockmarket is owned by individuals, as opposed to 18% in the UK). The Beardstown Ladies are a famous group of 16 women who proved very successful in investing. Their book – The Beardstown Ladies Common Sense Investment Guide – is a guide on 'ow to make money backed up with accounts of 'ow forming the club improved their lives. It must be pretty decent, the book's already sold 350,000 copies.

So what's keeping you? Get together with your friends and family, and form an investment club of your own. If nothing else it will keep you out of trouble and get you out the 'ouse on a regular basis.

THE CUT-OUT INVESTOR KIT

Nose to sniff out a good investment

X-ray glasses to see behind the blarney and rumours, and read between the lines in company accounts.

Belts and braces, for those who like to chose only the safest of safe investments.

ADAM'S INVESTMENT TIP
AWAITING THE BIRTH OF THE BULL

Bull markets are born on pessimism, grow on optimism and die on euphoria. The time of maximum pessimism may therefore be a good time to consider buying, as prices may be cheap. The time of maximum optimism is when prices are often high and heading for a fall, so it may therefore be a good time to consider banking your profits and selling.

Crystal ball to see into the future.

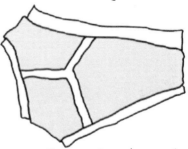

Spare pair of pants for those who like to chose very risky investments

EXPLAIN LORRAINE

So don't forget, you needn't be a millionaire to invest in shares. You just need a bit of dosh and a taste for adventure.

Keep your eyes peeled. You might 'ave an investment opportunity right on your doorstep. Take my mate Michelle for instance. She 'ad a building site opposite 'er 'ouse, noticeable for two things – the deafening noise and the drop dead gorgeous geezer who carried the bricks around. After making numerous efforts to meet 'im, she eventually struck lucky, only to go right off 'im. 'Owever, this brief liaison furnished 'er with information on 'ow quickly the building went up, the name of the company and 'ow many sites it 'ad. She promptly bought some shares, which did very nicely thankyou very much, and she laughed 'er way to the bank.

Another example is the Beardstown Ladies, a famous American investment club. The Beardstown Ladies noted that a certain make of washing machine broke down less often than other makes (there's not much else to talk about in Beardstown apparently). So they bought some shares, which also did very nicely, and they likewise laughed their way to the bank.

The chapter in a nut shell

You can pick you own shares or invest in a trust where they pick them for you.

Don't invest what you can't afford to lose. Not only can share prices go up as well as down, they can rise and fall for no good reason. As Spock from Star Trek might say – "It just isn't logical Captain"

Always remember there's commission to pay on deals.

Do your homework. There are many ways of judging share values on P/E ratios and dividend yields. High dividend yields suggest high pay outs. High P/E ratio suggest the company's expected to grow. Net Asset Value (NAV) is the break up value of a company.

CHAPTER 3

Free & Easy

HOW TO GET FREE PERKS WITH YOUR SHARES

I'm terrible about getting something for nothing – just like when you're at the supermarket with all that promotional rubbish in your hands – 'buy six get two free!' It's all too much trouble and I don't bother. So I can't say I'm all too concerned about shareholder perks. I feel much the same about them as the 'two pence off your groceries' voucher. Now Adam, on the other 'and, is a wise little man with a bulging wallet and very large feet. He just about fainted when I said I wasn't interested in shareholder discounts.

Leaving my wallet alone for a moment I think that shareholders' freebies are a whole new ball game. This isn't two pence off a tin of baked beans. You can save hundred of pounds with these sorts of discounts and what's more you don't have to fit them in your wallet or purse.

I tell you what, if you worked it out, you could buy shares in every aspect of your life. Let's 'ave a look. Start at the beginning: buying an 'ouse. Are there any shares that I could 'ave which would 'elp me setting up 'ome?

Well estate agents aren't known for being easy with their discounts, but some of the bigger companies can be generous. Barratt Developments, for instance, gives you £500 off for every £25,000 of the house/flat price. To get the shareholder discount you must have held 1,000 ordinary shares for 12 months before the completion of your house purchase.

Alright then – got me 'ouse. What about me DIY? Can I look after my 'ouse any cheaper if I get into any DIY companies? What I want is cheap DIY and a cheap man to do it for me.

Well the men don't come cheap, but the DIY might. Berisford, Meyer International and Sharpe and Fisher all offer discounts. Although they all have different rules about how many shares you need before qualifying for the discounts.

Alright then. I'm going to need some furniture.

What sort of furniture do you want?

What do you mean, what sort of furniture do I want? I want good furniture – a bit of class please Adam!

Alright. I'm not so sure about the class, Harvey Nichols doesn't offer discounts, but Courts does. If you have 100 ordinary shares for at least three months, Courts will give you 10% off the normal shop price of any of its bits and bobs.

Oooh goodie goodie! So what you're saying is that anything to do with the 'ouse I can get on the cheap. But what about me CELEBRATING my new 'ouse?

Well some frozen chicken legs come cheaper at Iceland. You get money-off vouchers with the annual set of reports. Not enough to keep you in food for the year but enough to knock a few pounds off the cost of toasting your new wealth and health.

OK – take your 'ealth. I mean, what are the possibilities of 'aving shares in a company which gives you, ooh I don't know – 20% off a wooden leg?

The only way you get money off a wooden leg is to get a shorter one, but if you want a health check you can get 20% off one of those at the Community Hospitals Group. You need at least 500 ordinary shares.

Well blow me – that's just about everything I want. How about World Peace?

Not with a discount I'm afraid.

CALLING ALL SHAREHOLDERS...
...NOW HEAR THIS

Most companies which offer a discount require shareholders to have a minimum amount of shares for a minimum period of time. So you can't just pop round the corner and buy a single share and then get 10% off a flight to the Caribbean. But some companies are more generous and offer discounts to all shareholders, even the tiny weeny ones. It is not possible to give all the details here and discounts are not usually valid in conjunction with other discount offers. Regulations also change from time to time, so it is important to check with the company before purchasing any shares.

AIRTOURS: The company owns a chain of over 700 travel agents and operates a charter airline. Shareholders are allowed 10% off Airtours holidays when booked through a special shareholders reservation service.

LEX SERVICE: This is a car distribution, servicing and leasing company. It offers occasional discounts to shareholders but very much on an ad hoc basis.

SHARPE & FISHER: The company supplies home building products on a wholesale and retail basis. Shareholders should receive up to £50 worth of vouchers, which are sent out with the annual report. The vouchers can only be used to pay tradesmen who themselves have accounts with the company. They cannot be used for cash purchases directly from Sharpe and Fisher branches. The vouchers are dependent on a minimum spend. There is no minimum number of shares you need to have before qualifying for the discount.

COATS VIYELLA: A textile and clothing company which has been going since 1784 producing a wide range of products from thread to finished garments. Shareholders receive a single voucher for 20% off purchases in independent Jaeger (gents & ladies) or Viyella (ladies) shops. No minimum share holding required to qualify for discount.

GENERAL ACCIDENT: Shareholders and immediate families living in the same house/flat are entitled to a discount of 10% on personal insurance bought directly from a General Accident branch. No minimum share holding required to qualify for discount.

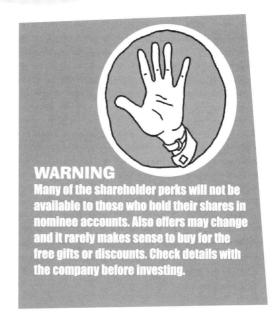

WARNING
Many of the shareholder perks will not be available to those who hold their shares in nominee accounts. Also offers may change and it rarely makes sense to buy for the free gifts or discounts. Check details with the company before investing.

Frozen peas, frozen pies and frozen prices at Iceland

ICELAND: Discount vouchers sent with the annual reports. Nothing too lavish but a nice little windfall. No minimum share holding required to qualify for discount.

LLOYDS CHEMIST GROUP: Not bad discounts vouchers these. They send out six vouchers which give 20% off the price of goods up to a certain limit. Because the group is quite large the vouchers can be used at variety of shops: Lloyds Chemists, Lloyds Supersave Drugstores, Lloyds Eyecare Centres, Holland and Barrett heath food stores, and John Bell & Croydon.

LADBROKE GROUP: A betting and hotel group. No free bets I'm afraid, but you can get 10% off Hilton accommodation and sometimes a free upgrade to a better class of room and discounts off food and drink. No minimum share holding required to qualify for discount.

GROUPE CHEZ GERARD: A restaurant chain in which all shareholders get free wine vouchers so that their steak and chips can slide down a little easier.

STANDARD CHARTERED: The bank offers shareholders, commission free travellers cheques. No minimum share holding required to qualify for discount.

WHITBREAD: The brewing and leisure group sends discount coupons with its annual report.

GREENE KING: Yet another brewing and retailing group which offers shareholders a discount off one case of wine.

See page 135 for an explanation of nominee accounts

EXPLAIN LORRAINE

The moral of the story is, if you're one of those people who doesn't mind taking the time and trouble to get something for nothing, there's always something for nothing to be 'ad.

A WORD IN YOUR EAR: There's a booklet published by the brokers Hargreaves Lansdown called 'Attractive Perks for UK Shareholders' which gives a much longer list of the perks you can get from 'olding particular shares. You can contact the company at:

Hargreaves Lansdown Asset Management Ltd,
Kendal House,
4 Brighton Mews,
Clifton,
Bristol BS8 2NX

The chapter in a nut shell

Don't invest in shares just for the perks. It rarely makes good financial sense.

If you already own shares, check with the company if it offers any shareholder perks. You may be missing out.

When you hold shares in a nominee account, you may not qualify for the perks.

CHAPTER 4

In the Pink

HOW TO READ & UNDERSTAND THE FINANCIAL PAGES

Like many of us, I bought British Telecom shares and then tucked them away thinking, "Fab! That's my little investment nest egg. I'll let them sit there like a pension scheme and wait." I felt my money was safe and one day I would clean up and reap the rewards. How naive!

Recently 'owever it crossed my mind (not a long journey) that I should pay more attention to my money matters. My plans, as far as my dosh was concerned, weren't good enough by a long shot. You've got to keep an eye on your shares. It's like buying a motor and running it into the ground. It needs its maintenance – a weekly wash and brush up, a monthly check on the tyres and a six monthly service. And shares are just the same. You've got to look after them because they don't look after themselves.

What would 'elp me no end is if I could check 'ow my shares are doing, understand what is meant by the various financial markets going up and down and 'ow to read the financial pages rather than seeing them as complicated bus or train timetables.

So Adam, get those little legs going, run up and down those pink pages and tell us what it's all about.

NEWSPAPER SHARE PAGES

Although the exact look of the information changes from one newspaper to another, they generally follow the same pattern. All of the shares quoted on the London Stock Exchange are listed under different industry sections. There's a section for everything from breweries, pubs and restaurants to paper, packaging and printing.

Having found the right industry section, look for the company name, which is listed alphabetically. Our share was issued by a television company and is therefore in the media section. The company is called *Chase Me*.

CHASE ME NOTES	PRICE	+ or -	52 week HIGH / LOW		MKT CAP £m	YLD Gr's	P/E
n	335	-4	350	320	3,000	2.8	30

The first thing you come to is the notes section. There won't always be something here but in our case there is an 'n'. You can find what this means by looking in the key, which is usually at the end of the share listings. In this example the 'n' means that a rights issue is expected to be made in the future.

CHASE ME NOTES	**PRICE**	+ or -	52 week HIGH / LOW	MKT CAP £m	YLD Gr's	P/E
n	**335**	-4	350 320	3,000	2.8	30

Now you would have thought the one simple thing to understand would be the price of the share. But the price listed in the above table is not exactly what it first appears. A share price may change many times over the course of the day. Newspapers list the mid-price at 4.30pm, when the shut sign is put on the stockmarket doors and official business ends for the day.

The mid-price is half way between the selling and the buying price. At any one time the price at which you buy shares is always higher than the price you get when you sell them. That's partly how the market maker (the person quoting the prices) makes money – they buy cheap and sell expensive, just like a shop owner does.

The price you have to buy at is called the **offer** price and the price at which you sell is called the **bid** price. The difference between the two prices is called the **spread**.

CHASE ME NOTES	PRICE	**+ or -**	52 week HIGH / LOW	MKT CAP £m	YLD Gr's	P/E
n	335	**-4**	350 320	3,000	2.8	30

The change in price is simply the difference in the price at the close of trade from one day to the next. A – (minus) sign means the price has dropped by 4 pence and a + (plus) sign means it has increased by 4 pence.

CHASE ME NOTES	PRICE	+ or -	**52 week HIGH / LOW**	MKT CAP £m	YLD Gr's	P/E
n	335	-4	**350 320**	3,000	2.8	30

The 52 week high and low figures show the highest and lowest price for *Chase Me* shares over the past year. Obviously if the difference between these two is very large, it gives you a clue as to how volatile the share price has been and how much money one might have made or lost over the past year.

CHASE ME NOTES	PRICE	+ or -	52 week HIGH / LOW	**MKT CAP £m**	YLD Gr's	P/E
n	335	-4	350 320	**3,000**	2.8	30

The MKT CAP stands for market capitalisation. This is a measure of how much the company is worth and it is calculated by adding up the price of all the shares which exist in the company. It gives you a chance to compare how big or valuable different companies are. *Chase Me* has a market capitalisation of £3,000 million pounds.

CHASE ME NOTES	PRICE	+ or -	52 week HIGH / LOW	MKT CAP £m	**YLD Gr's**	P/E
n	335	-4	350 320	3,000	**2.8**	30

The yield shows that for every £100 spent on *Chase Me* shares, the company would have paid £2.80 in dividends over the financial year, before tax. It is a guide to the company's dividend policy and can be a useful tool in estimating what you might make by waiting for the dividend cheque to come through the letter box.

However the yield is a calculation of past performance and does not predict the future, and used on its own it can be misleading. Be careful if you see a company with an unusually high dividend yield. Ironically the yield may have been pushed higher because the price of the shares have fallen.

CHASE ME NOTES	PRICE	+ or -	52 week HIGH / LOW	MKT CAP £m	YLD Gr's	**P/E**
n	335	-4	350 320	3,000	2.8	**30**

And finally P/E has nothing to do with physical exercise, it means the price/earnings ratio. The P/E ratio is calculated by finding out how many years it would take for the company's net profits after tax to equal the total value of all its shares. In our example, *Chase Me* would have to put aside 30 years' profits before it could equal the price of its shares. A high P/E ratio usually means the company is expected to grow quickly and a low P/E ratio means it's a bit of a slow coach.

It's a short-hand way of describing investors' confidence in the company and can be a useful way of judging the expected performance of a share, relative to other company's shares in the same industry. You might hear people talking about a company trading at 30 times earnings or trading at an earnings multiple of 30, all they mean is that the P/E ratio is 30.

WARNING
P/E ratios should be used for comparisons within the same sector. A media company's P/E ratio should not be compared with an industrial company's P/E ratio.

CHASE'S WARNING:
First reading may cause drowsiness and total confusion. No matter. Make yourself a nice cup of tea, sit down and read it again.

For a fuller explanation of how yields and P/E ratios works see Chapter 2 – StockPickers.

EXPLAIN LORRAINE

As long as I can remember the Financial Times pages 'ave always been pink. Why? Well a mate of mine reckoned it was something to do with the colour associated with the livery for the City. In the Coat of Arms the main colours were pink, red and green. Also, it was in the City that gentlemen, the 'chaps', first started wearing pink shirts, the ones with the white collars and cuffs. Funny that, they were even smart with saving money on their shirts – the point of this being that one only 'ad to change the collar and cuffs when they got a bit worn, and it didn't matter if the rest of the shirt 'ad faded a little. In other words, two wears out of one shirt – mean buggers. Actually, that's a bit 'arsh. They were only being practical.

Another theory on the subject of why the financial pages are pink, suggested to me by a director of Investment at Lehman Brothers, was to do with the practice of buying shares from your local store in America. Evidently there was a paper issued on a regular basis that would be pinned up by the cash desk. It was called the Pink Sheet and it contained all the relevant information concerning the local shares and investments. Needless to say, the paper was pink as the name suggests. So maybe this 'as a bearing on the tradition.

The chapter in a nut shell

Market Capitalisation is what it would cost to buy all the shares in the company at the current quoted price.

The price quoted in the papers is actually the mid price, which is half way between the selling and the buying price.

The 52 week high/low is the highest and lowest price the shares have reached over the past year.

The P/E is the price/earnings ratio and it shows how fast the company is expected to grow. A high P/E indicates fast growth, a low P/E indicates slow growth.

The dividend yield is the percentage of the amount you spent on the shares which is returned in the form of dividend payments. This is a calculation of past performance and is not a prediction of what will happen to dividend payments.

CHAPTER 5
Brokers

THE SERVICES THEY OFFER & HOW TO FIND THEM

"If it 'ainta broker, donta fix it."

If you want to buy or sell shares, or any of the products associated with them, you almost always have to go through a broker. It's no good I'm afraid turning up at the stock exchange with your share certificates in hand and touting for custom. First of all they wouldn't let you in and then even if they did, there would be no one there to buy the shares from you. Since 1986 trading in shares has taken place via special computer screens to which the professionals are the only ones to have access.

There are hundreds of brokers out there eager for your business, the problem is not finding a broker but deciding which broker you fancy. Your decision should be based on three things:

1 What sort of service you want.

2 The cost of the service.

3 Whether you like them or not.

Brokers offer three different types of service: execution only, advisory and discretionary.

1 An execution only service is one in which the broker does whatever you tell him. He'll buy and sell on your behalf and when you say jump, he says "how high?" This is the cheapest of the three types of broking services.

2 An advisory service is one in which the broker will give his opinion as to which shares should be bought and sold. A broker offering this service will buy and sell shares as well as advising on them.

3 A discretionary services places you in the hands of the broker and involves putting a great deal of trust in the broker's judgement. Under this arrangement, a broker will buy and sell whatever shares they feel are appropriate to your needs or requirements. They should contact you at regular intervals to tell you what they have done, but they can take investment decisions on your behalf, without referring to you.

Be warned – if you opt for this service you are giving the broker control of your finances. Make sure you understand the implications of this before you sign up to this service. If you decide this is for you, make sure you keep a careful and regular check on what they have done.

Of course brokers charge for the services they provide. Some charge more than others and the amount they charge varies according to the type of service they offer – so it does pay to shop around. The charges are based on a percentage of the value of every deal, so the commission fee increases with the price of the shares you are buying or selling. There is usually a minimum charge, so that if you are only dealing in small amounts of shares, check the minimum charge they make for dealing, it may be more important to you than the commission rate.

You should also watch out for other charges including special fees for trading in foreign shares, nominee account charges and management charges for operating advisory or discretionary services.

ADAM'S INVESTMENT TIP
DEALING WITH THE DIRECTORS

Directors of a company often have a shrewd understanding of their company's future prospects. Their share dealings can therefore be a reliable weather vane for future share prices. If a director is selling large quantities of his or her shares in the company, it's wise to ask why. Of course, the director may have personal reasons for needing cash and just because they're selling doesn't necessarily mean they think the share price will fall. But if you see a number of directors selling or buying shares in their company, it might give you food for thought.

Large director share deals are sometimes quoted in the national newspapers. A service is offered by a few companies like Directus which is based in Edinburgh, which keeps track of director share dealings.

FINDING A BROKER

You can get a full list of brokers by calling and speaking to the people from that easily remembered acronym – APCIMS, which stands for the Association of Private Client Investment Managers and Stockbrokers. Their directory gives a very comprehensive list of available brokers, details of brokers names, addresses, the services they offer and often how much they charge for advice and dealing. The directory is available free by writing to:

APCIMS,
112 Middlesex Street,
London E1 7HY

Of course the best recommendation is personal experience and if you already know a broker or a friend can recommend one to you, that is often the easiest and best place to go.

Most of the major banks offer broking services and an independent financial adviser should also be able to steer you in the direction of a broker they recommend. However, to help you, we have compiled our own list of some of the brokers offering services to small investors. Their inclusion in the table does not constitute a recommendation from us, and you should compare the price and service they offer before choosing your broker.

BROKER DIRECTORY

The following list covers a selection of brokers and investment managers who say they welcome small investors. *Their inclusion is not a recommendation.* Brokers often have more than one major office, and where this is the case we have tried to list two or three of them.

BARCLAYS STOCKBROKERS LTD
2nd Floor,
21 St Thomas Street,
London SE1 9RY
Tel: (0171) 403 4833

The Guild Hall,
57 Queen Street,
Glasgow G1 3DT

**BREWIN DOLPHIN
BELL LAWRIE LTD**
5 Giltspur Street,
London EC1A 9B
Tel: (0171) 236 4400

Sutherland House,
Castelbridge,
Cowbridge Road East,
Cardiff CF1 9AB
Tel: (0122) 344 999

Central Buildings,
11 Peter Street,
Manchester M2 4QR
Tel: (0161) 839 1651

BROADBRIDGE
Wellington Plaza,
31 Wellington Street,
Leeds LS1 4DL
Tel: (0113) 242 2211

12-14 Fountain Street,
Halifax HX1 1LX
Tel: (01422) 348 362

BWD RENSBURG
St George's House,
99-101 High Street,
Belfast BT1 2AH
Tel: (01232) 32 1002

11th Floor,
Bank House,
8 Cherry Street,
Birmingham B2 5AL
Tel: (0121) 643 0330

De Quincey House,
48 West Regent Street,
Glasgow G2 2RB
Tel: (0141) 332 9920

CHARLES STANLEY
25 Luke Street,
London EC2A 4AR
Tel: (0171) 739 7798

16 Northgate Street,
Ipswich,
Suffolk IPI 3DB
Tel: (01473) 225736

**FIDELTY BROKERAGE
SERVICES LTD**
Kingswood Place,
Tadworth,
Surrey KT20 6RB
Tel: 0800 222 190

**HARGREAVES LANSDOWN
STOCKBROKERS LTD**
Kendal House,
Brighton Mews,
Clifton,
Bristol BS8 2NX
Tel: (0117) 973 9902

HARRIS ALLDAY LEA & BROOKS
33 Great Charles Street,
Birmingham B3 3JN
Tel: (0121) 233 1222

HENDERSON CROSTHWAITE LTD
32 St Mary at Hill,
London EC3P 3AJ
Tel: (0171) 283 8577

The Coach House,
95a Hagley Road,
Edgbaston,
Birmingham B16 8LA
Tel: (0121) 455 0930

HILL OSBORNE & CO
Royal Insurance Building,
Silver Street,
Lincoln LN2 1DU
Tel: (01522) 513838

KEITH BAYLEY ROGERS & CO
Ebbark House,
93-95 Borough High Street,
London SE1 1NL
Tel: (0171) 378 0657

KILLICK & CO
45 Cadogan Street,
London SW3 2QJ
Tel: (0171) 384 4400

LLOYDS BANK STOCKBROKERS
48 Chiswell Street,
London EC1Y 4XX
Tel: (0345) 888 200

MIDLAND STOCKBROKERS
Mariner House,
Pepys Street,
London EC3N 4DA
Tel: (0171) 260 4298

NATWEST STOCKBROKERS
55 Mansell Street,
London E1 8AN
Tel: (0171) 895 5803

NEILSON COBBOLD
4 Water Street,
Liverpool L2 3UF
Tel: (0151) 236 6666

REDMAYNE-BENTLEY
Merton House,
84 Albion Street,
Leeds LS1 6AG
Tel: (0113) 243 6941

104 West Campbell Street,
Glasgow G2 4TY
Tel: (0141) 248 6941

12 Well Court,
London EC4M 9DN
Tel: (0171) 489 9955

THE SHARE CENTRE
St Peter's House,
Market Place,
Tring
Hertfordshire HP 23 4JG
Tel: 0800 800008

SHARELINK LTD
Cannon House,
24 The Priory Queensway,
Birmingham B4 6BS
Tel: (0121) 200 2474

JOHN SIDDALL & SON LTD
PO Box 499,
4 Norfolk Street,
Manchester M60 1DY
Tel: (0161) 832 7471

Mill Street,
4 New Concordia Wharf,
London SE1
Tel: (0171) 237 1090

**SINGER & FRIEDLANDER
INVESTMENT MANAGEMENT LTD**
21 New Street,
Bishopsgate,
London EC2M 4HR
Tel: (0171) 623 3000

55 Clathorpe Road,
Birmingham B15 ITL
Tel: (0121) 456 3311

**WALKER, CRIPS,
WEDDLE BECK PLC**
Sophia House,
76-80 City Road,
London EC1Y 2BJ
Tel: (0171) 253 7502

WISE SPEKE LTD
39 Pilgrim Street,
Newcastle Upon Tyne
NE1 6RQ
Tel: (0191) 201 3800

Cutler House,
3b Devonshire Square,
London EC2M 4YA
Tel: (0171) 617 2900

Sturge Court,
120 Wellington Street,
Leeds LS1 4LT
Tel: (0113) 245 9341

YORKSHARE LTD
Howard House,
6 Bank Street,
Bradford BD1 1HA
Tel: (01274) 736736

EXPLAIN LORRAINE

I think one thing to remember out of all this is that every broker is a salesman. They make money on the deal even if you don't, because they always get their commission.

Far be it from me to give you advice, but that discretionary service seems a bit off to me. Why work really hard to make your money, just to let someone else control it? As Obi Wan Kenobi would have said, "May the force be with you" (and don't give it away!).

The chapter in a nut shell

There's three types of broker services: execution only, where they'll do as you tell them; advisory, where the broker offers their advice on the best course of action; discretionary, where the broker does whatever he or she wants to with your shares. Make sure you opt for the service which best suits your needs.

As with everything, you pay for what you get. Different services charge different fees.

Never never be in awe of the broker. You have your best interests at heart so make sure your broker gives you the advice best suited to your needs. Where possible, go prepared.

CHAPTER 6
A Little Pep Talk

PERSONAL EQUITY PLANS
& WHAT THEY HAVE TO OFFER

*B*oy, if ever I was bored with hearing about anything, PEPs have to be the out and out winner. Last year, as this guide was desperately trying to be written (even though all the technology that I possessed was throwing every bloomin' trick in the book at me), all I kept hearing about day-in and day-out was flipping PEPs. Every paper that 'ad a financial section gave an awful lot of space to them, especially in the run up to the end of the financial year.

Now as far as I can understand you're allowed to put a set amount of money into a PEP every tax year. You have to work out which PEP is performing best, as well as which isn't charging a high management fee.

My accountant scared the life out of me by telling me that one of his clients 'as a PEP that has now lost money. Blimey, I said to him. If these bloomin' things are still an option, what are the chances of you making head or tail of them for me? Mind, last year I was a scared little bunny, when deciding whether or not I should invest in a PEP. You really do have to take care not to panic buy, as it were. It's so difficult knowing what and whose advice to take, especially when you're feeling like you're about to miss out on an opportunity.

Come on Adam, you're one of the few men I would trust. What advice would you give?

In the chorus line of attractive investments, one starlet seems to shine particularly brightly. Neither Beryl Bond, Gaia Gilts or Fiona Futures, nice as they are, have been taken to the public's heart, in quite the way that Patricia PEP has.

A PEP is a Personal Equity Plan and it is really no more than a scheme designed to encourage investment in the stockmarket. The encouragement lies in the form of tax breaks. But Patricia has grabbed the limelight on the investment stage and in the affections of the nation, in a way which could never have been dreamed of.

So what exactly are Patricia PEP's vital statistics?

She was born in 1986, the wild child of Nigel Lawson's budget of that year. PEPs were meant to help turn the UK into a "share owning democracy". That dream may not have been fully realised but PEPs have nonetheless become a very popular means of investing in the stockmarket.

ADAM'S INVESTMENT TIP
NOT JUST FOR THE RICH

You don't have to have a large sum of money to invest in a PEP. Instead of putting in a lump sum, you can invest regular small amounts.

In 1987 there were 270,000 PEPs taken out by investors. In the 1995-96 tax year that number had increased to about one and a half million PEPs with about five and a half billion pounds invested in them. The attraction of PEPs is that they are tax free.

There is no income tax to pay on the dividends of shares within the plan and no capital gains tax to pay on any of the profits. It sounds brilliant, doesn't it? But before you get enticed by the attractions of not paying the tax man anything, you should think carefully about whether the tax advantages are actually of any use to you.

That's because you can already earn a substantial amount of money in capital gains, without paying a penny in tax. In the 1997-98 tax year you could earn £6,500 in realised capital gains, without paying any capital gains tax.

In fact because the allowance is so generous, very few people pay capital gains tax. In 1985-86, there were 130,000 people paying capital gains tax. After the introduction of PEPs, that number fell so that by 1995 there was only 90,000 people paying the tax.

WARNING
PEPs are very good for some people, but they are not a financial panacea. There is often a feeling that these are saving schemes, but they are not. PEPs are investments in the stockmarket and the return is dependent on whether share prices are rising or falling. So PEP investments can lose money as well as make money.

But there are about one and a half million PEPs in operation and although investors can hold more than one PEP at a time, it seems that many people are interested in PEPs even though they seem to offer little or no benefit to them.

Even if you don't benefit from the capital gains tax break, the fact that there is no income tax to pay on dividends within a PEP sounds very appealing. But even this must be approached with caution. Because they are run by managers, anyone investing in a PEP has to pay a management charge. These fees can eat into much of the tax free benefits, especially for small investors and it is therefore wise to make sure you take the level of fees into account, when considering the advantages of investing in a PEP.

However if you have decided that a PEP is for you, you then face the task of choosing which PEP to plump for. There are hundreds of different PEPs advertised in the newspapers but they fall into one of six categories: general, single company, self select, unit trust, investment trust and corporate bond. You are allowed to hold many different types of PEPs at the same time but in each tax year you are allowed to open only one Single Company PEP and one other form of PEP.

ADAM'S INVESTMENT TIP PEP TALK

If you already own shares and wish to put them in a PEP, you can do so. In most cases however, you must sell them first and buy them back through the PEP provider. This means you will have to pay some extra dealing charges. It is therefore even more important that you make sure the tax advantages of a PEP outweigh the costs involved.

There is also a restriction on the amount you can invest in a single year. In 1997 the maximum permitted investment in each tax year was £9,000, split into £3,000 in a Single Company PEP and £6,000 in one of the other PEPs.

The **GENERAL PEP** consists of a variety of shares chosen by the PEP managers. Some PEPs offer the prospects of income. Other PEPs offer the prospect of capital growth and there are some PEPs which offer the prospect of both income and capital growth. Usually you can decide whether the dividends are sent to you or re-invested in the fund.

SELF SELECT PEPs give you the freedom to chose the shares, unit trusts and investment trusts in which you wish to invest. However, not all unit and investment trusts qualify for inclusion. Some PEP managers will restrict the amount of shares you can hold at any one time and you should be sure to check the charges for buying and selling shares within the PEP.

The **SINGLE COMPANY PEP**, as the name suggests, provide a vehicle within which you can invest in only one company's shares. Because it is impossible to spread your risk with only one company's share, this may not be the best choice for first time PEP holders or newcomers to the stockmarket. You can usually choose whether dividends are sent to you or whether they are re-invested in the fund.

UNIT TRUST PEPs have qualifying rules and do not allow you to invest in every unit trust available. The rules insist that you have a certain level of investment based in the UK or European Union. Your PEP provider can advise you on which trusts qualify for inclusion in this type of scheme. However a certain proportion of your investment can be made in non-qualifying investment trusts.

INVESTMENT TRUST PEPs also have qualifying rules about which investment trusts can be included in a PEP. The rules are based on the amount of investment made in the UK and Europe. However a certain proportion of your investment can be made in non-qualifying investment trusts.

CORPORATE BOND PEPs can include investments in corporate bonds, eurobonds, preference shares and convertible shares.

There are hundreds of adverts for PEPs and it can be hard to decide which PEP provider to chose. One way of helping you make up your mind up is to look at a PEP league table which will tell you how the different PEPs have performed in the past. Of course, just because a PEP has done well in the past doesn't mean it will do well in the future, but in the absence of other information or guidance, these tables do provide some useful information. A PEP performance chart is available from the financial advisers Chase de Vere, from their offices in London, Bath or Leeds. Tables are also often published in the financial magazines and newspapers.

ADAM'S INVESTMENT TIP
CHANGING YOUR MIND

After having chosen a PEP, there is sometimes a cooling-off period in which you can ask for your money to be returned if you decide that the PEP investment is in fact not for you. The period is limited and not all PEP schemes offer this facility. It is therefore important to check whether this is available and confirm the details before committing yourself to any PEP.

Darling, I had the personal organiser, then the personal trainer - now I just must have a personal equity plan.

EXPLAIN LORRAINE

Be careful, because newspapers often print what you assume to be an article, but is actually an advertisement for PEPs. Read the small print – check there isn't the word 'advertisement' in the top corner. There's nothing wrong with companies advertising. The difference is that ads will be pushing themselves and their products, whilst an article gives you unbiased advice. It's worth knowing the difference

The chapter in a nut shell

 PEPs are a tax free way of investing in shares and bonds.

You are allowed a Single Company and one other form of PEP each tax year.

The value of PEPs can go up as well as down.

Beware of the management fees charged by PEP providers.

CHAPTER 7

Timid Tessa

TAX EXEMPT SAVINGS ACCOUNTS & WHAT THEY HAVE TO OFFER

Timid Tessa is a shy creature, a woman happier staying at home than venturing out on a Saturday night and dragging herself back home in the early hours of Sunday. Not for her the weekend hangovers. Tessa prefers a cup of cocoa and an early-to-bed early-to-rise sort of life. That's because Tessa, or Tax Exempt Special Savings Accounts, are in most cases ways to save money rather than risk it on a stockmarket investment.

While Polly PEP was a child of Nigel Lawson's budget. Timid Tessa was a creation of the unassuming John Major, in his only budget as Chancellor of the Exchequer.

TESSAs provide a means by which investors can put away the bits of extra cash they might have, and store it in a savings account which can be kept open for five years. The difference between a TESSA and an ordinary bank or building society account is that the TESSA hides your money from the tax man.

If you have a lump sum to invest, you can place this directly into the account, as long as it is within the maximum investment limit. If you prefer, you can also drip-feed the account with a series of deposits. Over the five year period you may discover that there are much better TESSAs being offered than the one you have chosen. In this case it may be possible to change from one TESSA to another, but there may be high penalty charges for moving which can wipe out any benefit.

As long as your leave you money in for five years, everything is tax free. If you decide you want or need to withdraw any of the money you have deposited before the five year period has past, the scheme is automatically cancelled and all the interest you earnt within the account will be taxed. However, during the five year period you can withdraw the interest earnt on your savings. As long as this is the only thing you take out of the account, the withdrawal will be taxed but the account will not be cancelled. Of course if you leave all the interest in the account, it's all tax free.

So it's a fairly straight-forward little savings scheme and your only problem lies in deciding which TESSA to choose (most of the major banks and building societies offer TESSAs). Once a TESSA has matured, you can roll over the capital into a new Tax Exempt Special Savings Account .

If you think TESSAs are for you, there is a wide variety of them to choose from. You have a choice of TESSAs which pay a fixed rate of interest, a variable rate of interest, a rate which is guaranteed to rise by a set amount each year or even a TESSA which is linked to the performance of the FTSE 100 Index.

The returns offered by TESSAs are quoted in many of the weekend broadsheet newspapers and magazines like *MoneyFacts*.

Independent financial advisers will be happy, indeed keen, to sell you a wide range of TESSAs, or alternatively you can buy them directly from the TESSA provider. There is no difference in cost either way but in some cases it may be convenient and helpful to seek independent advice before committing yourself to this type of saving scheme.

EXPLAIN LORRAINE

Like PEPs, all the publicity for TESSAs started to get right up my nose – PEPs TESSAs, BESSAs and all.

'Tax Exempt Special Savings Accounts': just knowing what TESSA stood for immediately helped me out. I must say it made me wonder why I 'adn't got one, until once again I discovered all the variations available. You could say it's like my wardrobe of clothes. When it was small I found it much easier to decide what to wear. Now I have a dressing room, the decision about what to wear sends me batty, so I often say, "to hell with it" and stay in (just kidding! Don't get put off).

The chapter in a nut shell

TESSAs are Tax Exempt Special Savings Accounts.

In most cases their performance is more predictable than a PEP or a straight forward stockmarket investment.

They are available from a wide variety of banks and building societies.

You can make monthly deposits or dump a lump sum investment into a TESSA.

Watch out for charges for swapping between one TESSA and another before the maturity date.

CHAPTER 8

Trusting in Timothy

UNIT & INVESTMENT TRUSTS AND WHAT THEY HAVE TO OFFER

Timothy Trust puts on his racing gloves but doesn't drive a sports car. He gambles, but only once a year and he drinks only in moderation. That's because Timothy likes an occasional little flutter, but he takes great pains to limit the risk. That's why Timothy likes trusts.

Unit trusts and investment trusts are both stockmarket investments, so their value can fall as well as rise. But the major advantage of these trusts is that the risk is spread in a way which would be impossible for the small investor to do on their own.

If you invest in a single company's shares, one of the biggest problems you face is that a fall in its price has a major impact on the value of your total investment. The more shares you own in different companies, the less trouble you have when one share falls in price.

For instance, if you invest £1,000 in *Chase Me* shares and the shares halve in value, the value of your total investment has fallen by 50%. Big trouble and glum faces all round.

However if you have £1,000 invested in a unit trust which has 10 shares, only one of which is *Chase Me*, the fall in the price of the shares isn't quite as devastating. The 50% fall in the price of *Chase Me* shares only brings the value of your total investment down by 5%.

Unit and investment trusts therefore pool investors' money together and spread the money around a large number of companies. The individual investor can therefore own a small slice of a large spread of investments.

Of course if the price of a share rockets, they would have done better owning the share directly. But if the price of the share dives, then by holding it as part of a unit or investment trust, they don't suffer to the same degree.

All this sounds dreamy, but you do have to look out for management costs, which are charged to investors for the benefit of having their investments managed on their behalf. Although we've talked about trusts investing in shares, there are also trusts which invest in fixed interest products like gilts.

ADAM'S INVESTMENT TIP
INVESTING IN A TRACKER TRUST

According to River and Mercantile Investment Funds Ltd, of 124 unit trusts in the UK Equity Growth sector, there are only 12 which outperform the FTSE ALL Share Index over one, three and five years.

This fact has persuaded many people to invest in tracker funds, which copy the performance of the share index itself. These tracker funds also tend to charge lower fees than actively managed trusts.

So it's worth considering a unit trust which tracks the market as a whole. You can then add a few shares of your own by buying them separately. This will provide you with a good spread of investments and give you the fun of choosing your own shares as well.

You may hear that the difference between unit trusts and investment trusts is that one is open ended. Now this may sound like some nasty physical affliction, but it is in fact a description of how the trust's investment pool works.

If a unit trust sells more units to investors, it has more funds with which to invest. Access to the pool of money is never closed off and it grows and shrinks with the inward and outward flow of investors' cash. Unit trusts are therefore called open ended.

Investment trusts are quoted on the stockmarket, so instead of buying a slice of the investment pool, you buy a share in the company. In an investment trust, the size of the pool remains fixed. There are a set number of shares in the company and that cannot be enlarged or reduced according to demand.

Once the trust has been launched, access to the investment pool is closed and so investment trusts are called closed end funds.

Choosing which investment or unit trusts to go for can be a bit of a chore. But the main financial magazines have performance tables and an independent financial adviser will be able to sell you what they think is best. But it's not only the various providers which you have to decide between, it's also what sort of investment or unit trust is best suited to your needs.

There are many different types of trusts – from those which offer investment in small British companies to those which specialise in Japanese or American investments. But there is one special kind of trust which may need some careful explaining: the split capital trust.

That sounds painful. Adam. What exactly is a split trust?

Really it's a bit like having a tailor-made suit instead of an off-the-peg one. Ordinary trusts usually provide a bit of income in the form of dividends and a bit of capital growth as the value of the investment itself rises.

Split trusts separate these two elements. That means if you're not interested in income but are instead interested in a lump sum to pay off your bills, buy a house, pay for school fees etc., there's a trust which aims to provide capital growth. That way, you receive a lump sum when the trust is wound up.

On the other hand you may not have any dreams of packing the kids off to Eton, buying the semi-detached house or going on a world cruise and are more interested in getting a regular cheque through the post to help buy your groceries or pay the rent. In this case you should consider a split trust which aims to provide you with income rather than capital growth.

Well that's dead fab! What's the risk then? I mean. are some riskier than others?

There is always the risk that the value of your shares will fall. The additional risk with some trust investments is that you could be the last one to be paid any profits.

So fill us in on the incidentals then. What are you flogging me 'ere? I want names, dates, times!

Well here's a rough guide to what's out there.

Zero Dividend Preference Shares

DESCRIPTION: No income on offer here but you do get a fixed return on your capital. That means you know how much you'll be able to sell your shares for when they mature.

SUITABLE FOR: Cautious investors who want to know what's going to happen to their investments and want a lump sum when the investment matures.

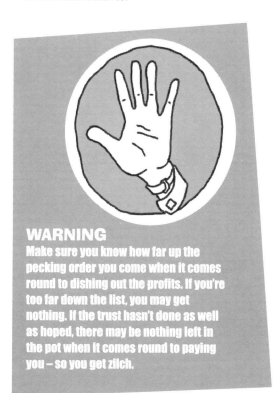

WARNING
Make sure you know how far up the pecking order you come when it comes round to dishing out the profits. If you're too far down the list, you may get nothing. If the trust hasn't done as well as hoped, there may be nothing left in the pot when it comes round to paying you – so you get zilch.

Stepped Preference Shares

DESCRIPTION: Income in the form of dividend payments which rise at a set rate throughout the length of the investment. You know how much you'll be able to sell your shares for when they mature.

SUITABLE FOR: Another investment for the relatively cautious investor. Best for those who want a bit of everything, income and a predictable level of capital growth.

Income Shares

DESCRIPTION: There are three types of income shares.

a: The traditional income share is designed to offer a high income. You also know how much you'll be able to sell your shares for when they mature.

b: The new income shares are designed to offer the prospect of high income but you don't know what you will get for your shares when they mature. You may be guaranteed a basic return with an additional top-up if there is any remaining money left in the fund. The flip side of the coin is that the shares may not be worth much when it comes to sell and so you actually make a capital loss.

c: Highly geared ordinary income shares are designed to offer a good income flow. However, whether or not you make a profit on the shares themselves depends entirely on whether there is any money left in the pot to buy the shares back from you once the fund is wound up. You will only be paid once the zero preference shareholders have been paid, and there may not be any money to give you. So be careful.

SUITABLE FOR: More experienced investors who are aware of the risks involved and are prepared to face them. As the name implies, this is mainly for those interested in income rather than capital growth.

Capital Shares

DESCRIPTION: Capital shares offer the potential but not the promise for large capital growth. One thing you are guaranteed is that you'll get no income during the life of the shares. The owner of the capital share receives a proportion of the remaining assets after the trust is wound up. Of course, as we've said before, if there's nothing left in the pot you won't get paid.

SUITABLE FOR: Experienced risk seekers in search of lump sums instead of income.

Units

DESCRIPTION: Some split trusts bundle their income and capital shares together, so you can get a fairly even mixture of capital growth and income.

Warrants

DESCRIPTION: A right, but not an obligation, to buy shares in the trust at a set price within a set period. If the right to buy is not exercised before the expiry date, they become worthless and so these are risky investments. Warrants are derivatives, which we will explain in Chapter 11.

WARNING
The devil's in the detail, and split trusts can be very complex. Unless you really know what you are doing, it is good to take independent advice before committing yourself to this kind of investment. We are only able to give an outline of these products here and specific offers may vary from one company to the next.

TRUST CATEGORIES

Category

Explanation

UK EQUITY GROWTH

Even though it's called UK Equity Growth, this doesn't mean all of its investments are in the UK – only a minimum of 80%. And as the name implies, the investments are chosen for their growth potential as opposed to their ability to generate a flow of income.

UK EQUITY INCOME

Must have at least 80% of assets in UK equities, which aim to offer a yield in excess of 110% of the FTSE All Share Index. The fund therefore seeks shares which produce good dividends.

UK GILT & FIXED INTEREST

At least 80% of its assets must be in UK gilts and fixed interest securities, just like the name implies.

UK SMALLER COMPANIES

This sort of trust must invest at least 80% of its funds in equities which form part of the Hoare Govett UK Smaller Companies Extended Index.

FINANCIAL AND PROPERTY

Trusts which have at least 80% of their investments in financial and property securities.

COMMODITY AND ENERGY

The magic number 80% rears its head again.
To qualify as a commodity and energy trust, 80% of its investments must be in commodity and energy trust securities.

MONEY MARKET

80% of assets must be in money market instruments.

INT'L EQUITY GROWTH

These trusts have at least 80% of their investments in equities aimed at producing growth.

INT'L EQUITY INCOME

Must have 80% of its investments in equities which aim to have a yield of over 110% of the FT Actuaries World Index.

INT'L FIXED INTEREST

Must have at least 80% of funds in fixed interest stocks. They can be called international even if they have more than 80% of those stocks in just one geographical area. The only exception to this rule seems to be if the funds are invested in the UK, in which case it would be called a UK gilt and fixed interest fund.

COUNTRY TRUSTS

Like a North American trust or a Japanese trust, these must have at least 80% of their investments in securities in the named country.

FUND OF FUNDS

Very much a dog chasing its own tail here. This is a unit trust which invests in other unit trusts.

INVESTMENT TRUST UNITS

Trusts which are only allowed to invest in the shares of investment trust companies.

CONVERTIBLES

Trusts which have at least 60% of their assets in convertibles.

WARNING

For those of you who want to buy British, be careful. So-called UK funds need have no more than 80% of their assets in the UK and 20% may be invested abroad.

International trusts may not be that international. A trust with 79% of its assets in just one country may still officially be called international.

EXPLAIN LORRAINE

Put it this way Adam, this is 'ardly the rollercoaster ride of straightforward share investment – champagne one day and cracked mugs the next. This kind of investment evens out the 'ighs and lows. It's precisely the sort of thing I should be doing at my time of life, by taking things more gently. 'Owever you can still lose money as well as make it.

A LITTLE WORD IN YOUR EAR: You can get a range of free fact sheets from the Association of investment trust Companies. Contact:

Eleanor Burton, AITC,
Park House 6th Floor,
16 Finsbury Circus,
London EC2M 7JJ
Telephone: (0171) 588 5347

The chapter in a nut shell

Unit and investment trusts allow the small investor to spread their risks by investing in a large selection of companies.

Be aware of management costs which can eat into your profits.

It may reduce your risks by spreading the load but it can also reduce your profits.

Ordinary trusts aim to provide you with income (dividends) and capital growth (value of investment).

A split capital trust gives you the option of income or capital growth. Shares available include: Zero dividend preference shares, stepped preference shares, income shares, capital shares, units and warrants.

CHAPTER 9

The Name's Bond

GOVERNMENT & CORPORATE BONDS
AND WHAT THEY HAVE TO OFFER

James Bond 007
meets Treasury Bond
008.75 in a story
guaranteed to provide
interest.

onds are issued by both governments and companies. The bonds issued by companies are called corporate bonds and those issued by the British government are called gilts or gilt-edged securities. Gilts and corporate bonds are both forms of IOUs and they are the means by which government and companies can raise money to fund their spending plans.

The bond holder lends the government or company an agreed sum of money. In return the bond holder receives a fixed rate of interest for a set period of time. Once that period has elapsed, the bond holder expects the loan to be paid back.

Anyone who doesn't fancy waiting around to collect the loan can sell the bond to someone else. The new owner of the bond will collect any interest which is yet to be paid and when the time comes, they will collect the money owed from the original loan.

WARNING
Despite being called gilt-edged, there is no guarantee you can sell a bond for the same price you bought it. Prices fluctuate on a daily basis and unless you bought at the issue price and hold the bond until it matures, you do not know at what price you can sell. If you buy a corporate bond, make sure the company is creditworthy. If the company goes bust, they may not be able to pay the loan back.

TYPES OF BOND

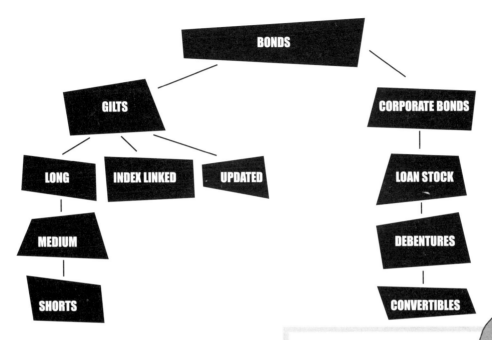

Ordinary gilts come in three forms: long, medium and short. This refers to the period of time which elapses between the bond being issued and the loan being repaid. Short bonds last for under five years, mediums are for between five and fifteen years and longs last for over 15 years. Then there are the undated gilts, which have no redemption date. That means there is no promise to repay the original loan at any specific time. In this case, interest is paid regularly but the original loan is only repaid when the government decides to. Since few organisations like paying loans back unless they have to, a lot of these undated gilts have been around for a long, long time and many exist from the 1940s.

Corporate bonds come in two main varieties: loan stock and debentures. Both operate in similar ways but debentures are backed by a company's assets while loan stock are not always secured on any assets. Like gilts, corporate bonds pay a

ADAM'S INVESTMENT TIP

There is no capital gains tax to pay on profits made by selling government bonds. Those investors who are trying to limit their tax liability should take account of this in their investment planning.

fixed rate of interest and they aim to repay the original loan. However, many companies get into financial trouble and some go bankrupt. Under these circumstances the company may not be able to meet its obligations to the bond holder. Corporate bonds are therefore riskier than gilts and before investing in any corporate bond, you should make sure that you are happy with the credit worthiness of the company to which you are lending your money. Because of the risk involved, corporate bonds tend to pay higher rates of interest than gilts.

Just to complicate matters, companies can also issue convertible bonds. These operate like ordinary bonds but under certain circumstances they offer the holder a chance to convert the bond into shares. A convertible bond is therefore similar to having two products at once, a corporate bond and a share option.

There are other types of bonds than those discussed here, but most operate along similar lines. To work out whether a bond is a good investment for you, you have to understand how bond prices work. The basic pricing principle is the same for corporate bonds and gilts and this is how you will find them listed in the *Financial Times*.

NOTES	YIELD		PRICE £	+ or −	1994/95	
	INT	RED			HIGH	LOW
TREAS 14% 2004	13%	5%	110	-1/16	115	107

The notes section gives you the name of the bond, the coupon rate and the redemption date. This is a treasury bond (another name for gilt or gilt-edged stock). The coupon rate is 14% and it is redeemable in 2004.

The coupon rate is the interest paid on the original sum borrowed. Since the issue price of all gilts is £100, the interest paid is 14% of £100. This means that the government has agreed to pay £14 a year until the year 2004

when it will pay back the original £100 loan. Even if you pay more than £100 to buy the bond, the government will still only pay £14 a year and will only repay £100.

At a time when interest rates are generally 6-7% this may sound brilliant – but it's not as good as it seems. The real rate of interest paid on this investment is much lower than 14% as you can see if you look under the yield column.

NOTES	**YIELD**		PRICE £	+ or −	1994/95	
	INT	**RED**			HIGH	LOW
TREAS 14% 2004	**13%**	**5%**	110	-1/16	115	107

Now look at the price column, you can see that this particular bond sells at £110, which is more than its issue price of £100. Once you've bought the bond, you receive £14 a year for your £110 outlay. If you do the maths you'll find that means an interest rate of 13% is being paid, but to save you doing all that hard work the paper has done it for you and the effective interest rate is listed under YIELD INT, meaning the interest yield.

The government will pay back the loan in the year 2004, but they will only pay back the

£100 they originally borrowed. As we have just said, you have paid £110 for the bond so will make a loss of £10 when the bond is repaid. You have to take that into account when considering whether this is a good investment. But there is no need to do any fancy calculations because again the newspaper has done it for you. The figure listed under YIELD RED (which means redemption yield) is the rate of return you will earn if you buy the bond at this price, hold it until the year 2004 gathering the interest on the way and then collect the original loan when it's repaid.

As you can see the redemption yield is substantially below the coupon rate or even the interest yield, and it is a more realistic picture of the returns available to an investor who holds the bond until it is repaid. This is the rate you should compare with other investments available to you, before you make an investment decision.

NOTES	YIELD		**PRICE £**	+ or –	1994/95	
	INT	RED			HIGH	LOW
TREAS 14% 2004	13%	5%	**110**	-1/16	115	107

The price of the bond is quoted in pounds.

If the interest rates available to investors fall to just 1%, then our bond which offers a redemption yield of 5%, looks very attractive. Lots of people will want to buy the bond and as a result, its price will rise. As the price rises the interest yield and redemption yield will fall because you are having to pay more for the same amount of interest income. It is for this reason that the price and interest rates go in opposite directions: as one rises the other falls.

NOTES	YIELD		PRICE £	**+ or –**	**1994/95**	
	INT	RED			**HIGH**	**LOW**
TREAS 14% 2004	13%	5%	110	*-1/16*	*115*	*107*

The plus and minus column shows how much the price has changed in the last trading day. The high and low figures show the maximum and minimum price reached over the last year.

ADAM'S INVESTMENT TIP
BUYING THROUGH THE POST OFFICE

Gilts can be bought through a stockbroker or through the post office. The advantage of buying through the post office is that the commission is lower and the interest paid on gilts is gross. That means it's paid without tax being deducted. Although tax payers will eventually have to pay tax on their income from gilts, it can be advantageous to be paid gross because the money lies in your bank account and you earn interest on it before you have to hand it over to the tax man.

Corporate bonds cannot be bought at the Post Office and must be purchased through a stockbroker.

EXPLAIN LORRAINE

The national debt is the amount of money the government 'as borrowed to finance its spending. Have you ever thought about the national debt? No, neither 'ave I. But the other day I was in the City 'aving lunch with Charles Galt and Victor Farhi at Lehman Brothers (to die for!), and while I was there I took the opportunity to go and visit another dear friend of mine, Chris Dereham. He's a dead good egg with the patience of a saint, and we often chat with the intention of broadening my knowledge of finance and the like. We 'ad a fab old time, and God only knows why, but we got onto the national debt.

As we're into bonds, and that's what funds the national debt, I will now attempt to give you the gist of it. Quite frankly, I found it fascinating.

In the UK the national debt is about 400 thousand million pounds – a tidy little sum eh? This is a figure which respective governments conveniently forget to talk about (I wouldn't either if I owed that much!).

We've already discussed gilt edged stocks, which are certificates issued by the government with a nice guaranteed return. They mature (becoming redeemable) on a particular date in the future.

ADAM'S INVESTMENT TIP
GETTING A HIGH RATE OF INTEREST

If interest rates are high and you think they will fall in the future, it can make sense to buy long dated new issues of gilts. This commits the government to paying you high rates of interest for years to come. Even if the general level of interest rates fall in the future, you are guaranteed to get a relatively high level of interest.

However, there is a risk that your prediction is wrong and interest rates don't fall but rise. In this case you may have done better to have invested elsewhere. So this strategy does depend on making judgments about what you think will happen to interest rates in the future.

If you bought, say, £1000 worth of the 2010, 5¹/₅% stock (new ones you can purchase in 1997), that means you would get 5¹/₅% return on your money each year until the year 2010 when they matured. This kind of investment is often taken out by pension funds who are looking for longterm guaranteed income. Let's face it, who would be better to guarantee your money than the government of the day?

I suppose you could say it's an overdraft facility which the government 'as, and very 'andy it is too. And it's us who gives them that facility (does that make us a little bank?).

What 'appens, you might ask, when it comes to maturing the 2010 5¹/₅% gilt edged stock? Or indeed the 1997 6¹/₅% stock? They 'ave to pay it back of course. Which raises the question: where on earth do they get all the money from? Bear in mind that according to 'ow many were originally issued, this could be way up in the 'undreds of millions. The final bill could be an 'efty one – and that's putting it lightly.

Any guesses? Dip into the petty cash? Sell the navy? Venture a sizable sum on the 3:30 at Cheltenham?

NO!

It's easy if you 'ave a little think about it. They issue the 2025 gilt edged stocks, a £100 millions' worth. And no prizes for guessing who buys them. Yes, you've got it. Us. We've come full circle.

The chapter in a nut shell

 Bonds are IOUs issued by government and companies

 Corporate bonds are issued by companies and gilts or gilt edged securities are issued by the British government.

 Convertible bonds are issued by companies. They are a two-in-one product and consist of a bond and a share option.

 The redemption yield is the best judge of the interest rate paid by a bond.

 If you're buying a corporate bond, make sure you're happy with the creditworthiness of the company.

CHAPTER 10
Ethical Investments

"I said profit, not prophet !"

I was very interested to read about the existence of ethical funds. This may sound stupid, but I really 'ad no idea that an ethical fund was available. It sounds like a contradiction in terms. But in these days of better social awareness (we 'ope) I thought I'd find out a little bit more.

Ethical funds first started in the UK in the mid-1980s and 'ave now attracted over £1 billion of investors' cash. What's more, they 'aven't performed too badly at all. We're still behind the US in the number of ethical funds around, but we are looking decidedly more aware of this type of investment than continental Europe.

So what does 'ethical' mean? Well 'opefully it means avoiding investing in companies that are involved in arms sales, environmental pollution, nuclear power, alcohol, tobacco, cruelty to animals, pornography and gambling. Of course by blacklisting these

things, particularly arms, tobacco and alcohol, it does mean that you're going to miss out on some of the most prestigious shares. But ethical funds 'ave been performing well despite avoiding some of the best known and largest of our companies.

So anyway, what's all this about then? I set Adam on the trail to dig out the facts and figures. 'Ere 'e goes.

Thousands of people put their savings into PEPs, TESSAs, bonds and equities with one thing in mind: to make themselves richer. But many people are now leafing through their Big Book of ethics in search of investments which, while making a profit, take care to invest in ethically correct ventures.

The first thing to ask about moral or ethical investments is whose ethics are they? That's because there are no set ethical criteria for investment funds and their investment policies vary, according to their own particular priorities and views. So even if you are keen to invest in a way which benefits the environment and the population, don't just plump for any ethical fund. Make sure their ethics match yours.

Just because you invest in an ethical fund, bank or building society, it doesn't necessarily mean you have to accept a lower profit. But with so many ethical trusts on the market it can take some time to find one which matches your particular concerns.

A helping hand is offered by EIRIS – the Ethical Investment Research Service. It will supply a list of independent financial advisers who specialise in ethical investments. If you already have your own, home-made, share portfolio and want to check how ethical your investment strategy is, it will examine the portfolio for you for a small charge.

Ethical policies can change of course, but here is a quick guide to the policies of the major ethical banks and building societies as they stood in mid 1997.

The Co-Operative Bank

▶ Will not invest in or supply financial services to any regime or organisation which oppresses the human spirit, takes away the rights of individuals or manufactures any instruments of torture

▶ Will not finance the manufacture or sale of weapons to countries with an oppressive regime

▶ Will not speculate against the pound

▶ Will not provide financial services to tobacco product manufacturers

▶ Will not invest in any business involved in animal experimentation for cosmetic purposes

▶ Will not support any person or company using exploitative factory farming methods

▶ Will not engage in business with any organisation involved in the production of animal fur

▶ Will not support any organisation involved with blood sports

The Co-Operative Bank has the most wide ranging and detailed ethical policies of the major ethical bank and building societies. A full and more comprehensive explanation of its policies is available from the bank by writing or phoning:

The Co-Operative Bank,
1 Balloon Street,
Manchester M60 4EP
Tel: (0161) 829 5436

The Ecology Building Society

The Ecology Building Society's main concern is to finance the purchase of ecologically sound buildings or companies involved with ecological projects. Deposits in the building society will therefore help to fund the purchase of:

▶ Small scale workshops

▶ Derelict houses

▶ Small businesses with an ecological flavour, like paper recycling

▶ Houses with energy saving or energy efficient features

▶ Organic small holdings

▶ Properties which will help promote the life of small communities

More details can be found by contacting:
The Ecology Building Society,
18 Station Road,
Cross Hills, Near Keighley,
West Yorkshire BD20 7EH
Tel: (01535) 635933

Triodos Bank

Although the Co-Operative Bank issues the longest and most detailed ethical policy, most of it describes what the bank won't do. The Triodos Bank stands this on its head and describes what it *will* do. Its policy statement says the bank will invest "only in organisations and businesses with social and environmental objectives." Money deposited here will therefore help finance loans to:

▶ Environmental initiatives

▶ Community services social housing

▶ Projects in the developing world

▶ Charity projects in fields such as education, special needs, complimentary health care, spiritual and religious groups, the arts.

The Triodos Bank is a Dutch bank which operates in the UK. Further details of its policies can be obtained by contacting:
Triodos Bank,
Brunel House,
11 The Promenade,
Clifton,
Bristol BS8 3NN

Lorraines's Little Somethings

THE LOW INTEREST RATE TRAP

If, like many people you've been wooed into a building society account with the promise of 'igh interest rates, BE WARNED! John Stapleton (the man who used to present Watchdog and now fronts The Time & The Place) very kindly gave me this little word of advice.

He realised that the interest rates on an account 'e'd opened in the distant past (when the rates were very good), 'ad dropped considerably. He'd received no notice of the change. When 'e quizzed the building society, they explained that their policy was not to write to the individuals concerned, but to put up a notice of the change of rates in the building society office.

It was nice little number. Building societies were attracting new customers to certain savings accounts by offering 'igh interest rates. These accounts would then slowly be run down, i.e.: the interest rates would be gently lowered over a period of time. Meanwhile, the building society was bringing in new customers with other savings accounts under new names and similarly attractive 'igh interest rates, using one account to finance the other.

Like most of us, I think, John rarely visited 'is society, so the change in rates 'ad sneaked up on 'im. When 'e did realise what 'ad 'appened, it was a nasty surprise.

John explained that Watchdog researched and exposed this practice, and although the building societies 'ad cleaned up their act, it was still well worth keeping an eye on interest rate changes.

Cheers John! We'll watch out for that one in future!

The Catholic Building Society

While it does business with a wide range of people and organisations, it particularly likes to lend to women and the low paid.

The building society also refuses to invest in the stockmarket. More information can be obtained by contacting:

Catholic Building Society
7 Strutton Ground,
Westminster,
London SW1P 2HY
Tel: (0171) 222 6736/7

EXPLAIN LORRAINE

Wouldn't it be great if we could all put our money where it would not only benefit our pocket, but the community and environment as a whole? Well, I've learnt that we can. Look at the power of the 'ousewife when it comes to the supermarkets and what's become available on the shelves. Years ago you couldn't get organic fruit and veg, and back then who would 'ave thought you'd be able to buy re-cycled toilet paper one day? Next time you're in the supermarkets take a butchers at the coffee section. You'll see Cafe Direct, a company that buys from producers in Africa and Latin America and guarantees them a fair price (a useful bit of information for those of you interested in 'elping the developing world in some small way). Through the power of money we are already re-shaping the world.

There are many possibilities for those who feel strongly enough, and who 'ave enough collective purchasing power to change things. You can – as they say – put your money where your mouth is. What price would we put on doing more with our savings than simply making a few extra quid for ourselves – where the word 'saving' applies to a darn sight more than our bank balance?

A LITTLE WORD IN YOUR EAR: If you want to invest in ethical shares or want to check how ethical your existing share portfolio is, contact: EIRIS – the Ethical Investment Research Institute, Bondway Business Centre, 71 Bondway, London SW8 1SQ

It will supply a list of independent financial advisers who specialise in ethical investments. It will charge for this service.

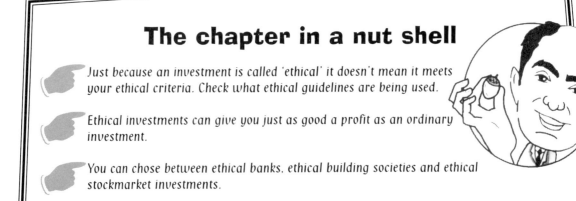

The chapter in a nut shell

Just because an investment is called 'ethical' it doesn't mean it meets your ethical criteria. Check what ethical guidelines are being used.

Ethical investments can give you just as good a profit as an ordinary investment.

You can chose between ethical banks, ethical building societies and ethical stockmarket investments.

CHAPTER 11

Rocket Science Investing

THE RISKS & REWARDS OF INVESTING IN DERIVATIVES

"Space isn't remote at all. It's only an hours drive away, if your car could go straight upwards."

Fred Hoyle,
British Astronomer

If gilt edged bonds are the kids' chemistry set, derivatives are the rocket science end of the investment world. Derivative markets can be complex, volatile and explosive. But they can also be very profitable and ironically although they can be dangerous, they can also be used to reduce risk.

Alright, so they're flash, but what exactly are they?

Food For Thought

Well just as juice is derived from oranges and gravy is derived from meat, so derivatives are derived from shares, currencies and commodities. There are two main types of derivatives: futures and options.

The Future Belongs To Me

Yes it's true, you can actually own a piece of the future. A future's contract is an agreement to buy or sell something at some time in the future at a price you fix today. This is a handcuffed commitment and ties you to a course of action.

You buy a futures contract when you think the price of something is about to rise, the contract allows you to buy tomorrow at today's prices.

Lorraines's Little Somethings

'Ang on Adam. As my dad used to say while he was serving at Her Majesty's Pleasure, there's always a way out. And he should know, he jumped the wall twice. Even with a futures contract you're not quite handcuffed – you can sell your futures contract to someone else.

 IF YOU'RE NOT INTO COMMITMENT, don't buy futures. As we said futures contracts commit you to a course of action. If you don't like commitment, opt for an option. Options give you the same opportunity as futures but you have a choice about whether to buy or sell at a specific price, you are not obliged to do so. So if futures contracts are handcuffs, options are the keys.

 LIVING DANGEROUSLY – is something farmers have never liked. In fact they hated it so much, that in the 19th century they developed derivatives as a way of reducing the risk of fluctuating crop prices. The farmers could sell their produce before it was even harvested. The farmer would therefore know that he had not only found a buyer for his produce but he had also fixed the selling price.

The farmers were therefore as happy as Larry. They knew what was going to happen in the future to their crops and to their bank balances. And the consumers could rest easy

as well because they knew that whatever happened to the market price of farm produce, they had bought themselves a guarantee that the cost of munching on their bread, pork or beef was already fixed.

Of course if the farmers had held out, they may have found they'd been able to sell at a higher price. Had the consumers waited, they may have found out they could have bought at a lower price. Dealing in futures and options contracts didn't guarantee anyone the best deal but it did guarantee everyone peace of mind.

Peace of Mind

THAT'S LIFFE – indeed that is LIFFE, the London International Financial Futures Exchange. It is the name of the market in the UK which deals with financial derivatives.

FILL YOUR BOOTS without dipping deeply into your pockets. That is the advantage of investing in derivatives. You can make huge profits with only a small investment, but of course you can also make huge losses. The reason for this volatility is something called the margin payment. Doing a deal on the margin means you only pay a fraction of the cost of the products when you strike the deal and you can delay paying the rest until later. If the price of the product goes up, you can even arrange to sell the futures or options contract to someone else. In that way you can make enormous profits with only a small outlay.

THE DERIVATIVE CARTOON STRIP

Mr Portly needs some lard to keep his hungry family happy over the winter months. He's worried that the price of lard may go up in the winter and so he's keen to reserve his order of lard at a fixed price which he knows he can afford.

Along comes a lorry with £10,000 worth of lard in its container. Mr Portly doesn't need the lard now but he wants to make sure he can get it when the time comes.

Instead of buying the lard, which would mean he would have to store it until winter, he buys an options contract. This reserves the lard for him and give, him the right to buy it in three months' time, at the current market price. But because he only pays on the margin, the contract costs Mr Portly an initial 10% of its value, which is £1,000.

Mr Portly exercises his option to buy the lard at £10,000 and immediately sells it on to the super-markets for £15,000.

Unexpectedly, Delia Smythe comes out with a new lard cookbook. The supermarkets are swamped with lard-mad shoppers. You can't get lard for love nor money and so the price rises. Mr Portly's lorry of £10,000 worth of lard is now worth £15,000.

To Recap

INITIAL OUTLAY: £1,000
PROFIT: £15,000 – £11,000 = £4,000
% PRICE CHANGE: 50%
% RETURN: 400%

Although prices rose by only 50% Mr Portly made a profit of 400% of his initial outlay. That's the beauty of derivatives.

THE PRODUCTS

Although there are two main types of derivatives – the big parents of the derivative family being options and futures – there are scores of baby offspring.

Call Options are the right to buy at a specific price in the future. If you buy a Marks and Spencer 500 April Call, it means you have the right to purchase one M&S share at 500 pence before the end of April. The option doesn't come free of course, and in our example it costs 33 pence. Therefore the moment Marks and Spencer's shares have risen above 533 pence, you can make a

profit. In the jargon of the market you are 'in the money.'

If the shares rise to a price of 600 pence, you will still be able to buy them at 500 pence and then immediately sell them at the higher price. You've therefore pocket 100 pence. If you then deduct the cost of the option itself, you will find that you have made a profit of 64 pence.

If the shares fell to 400 pence it would be silly to use your option to buy them at 500 pence, so you just wouldn't use it. But you have limited the size of your loss to the cost of the option itself, which is 33 pence.

Put Options are the other side of the coin, they provide their owners the right to sell at a specific price in the future. You would normally buy a Put option if you thought the value of the underlying investment was about to fall. If you bought a Marks and Spencer 500 pence April Put, you'd have bought the right to sell those shares at 500 pence at any time until April. The Put option isn't free and in this example it costs 25 pence.

If the shares fall to 400 pence, you are still able to sell them for 500 pence. So you buy them at 400 and sell them at 500 and pocket 100 pence. Deduct the price of the put option itself and you've made 75 pence profit.

If the market price rose to 600 pence, you would of course find plenty of people willing to buy the M&S share from you at 500 pence, but you would lose money by selling at that price and so you just wouldn't use your Put option. But once again, you have limited the size of your loss to the cost of the Put option, which in this case is 25 pence.

Trading Options is also possible. There is no need to actually keep the option contract until you use it or tear it up.

Futures contracts originated because of the needs of farmers to guarantee they had a market for their produce. The contracts where therefore based on real, tangible products like wheat. However many futures contracts now deal in much less tangible products like those listed below.

FTSE Futures allow people to bet on the future direction of the FTSE Index. If you think the market will fall in value, you buy a FTSE future which allows you to sell the index at the current price. The futures contract therefore protects you from any fall in the value of the market.

Currency Futures allow businesses with a lot of international trade to protect themselves against large movements in the exchange rate. Buying a currency futures contract fixes the exchange rate for a specified period of time and you therefore know that even if foreign currency values rise in relation to the pound, you can buy the currency at the old rate.

Swaps are the grown-up equivalent of the playground game, swapsies. Remember when you had four stickers with Bobby Moore on them but couldn't get one with George Best for love nor money? Then you found a friend who had loads of George Best stickers and no Bobby Moore ones, so you swapped. Well the City still plays those types of games.

For Example: Mr UK is a well known businessman in Britain. He wants to expand into the American market and therefore needs to borrow dollars. Mr UK could get a cheap loan in Britain. However, because he is unknown in America, he doesn't find it easy to get a loan there, and would therefore have to pay a high interest rate for any dollars that he borrowed.

Mr USA is a well known businessman in America and he wants to expand into the UK market and therefore needs to borrow pounds. Mr USA could get a cheap loan in America. HOWEVER being unknown in Britain, he doesn't find it easy to get a loan here and would therefore have to pay a high interest rate for any pound he borrowed.

Each has an advantage in borrowing money at home. So that's exactly what they do. Mr UK borrows pounds and Mr USA borrows dollars and (yes you've got it), they just swap the currencies. In that way they have both borrowed at low rates of interest and got the foreign currency they want. And that's the game of swapsies.

Lorraines's Little Somethings

DERIVATIVE PRODUCTS

My accountant, a very astute geezer, was dead chuffed when 'e told me this little story. It seems 'e put down a £2,000 deposit on an order for a Mercedes SLK when the car was barely off the drawing board. About six years later 'e was informed that the car was ready for delivery. As often 'appens with jam jars of this calibre (so I'm told) no sooner 'ad it been launched than every Tom Dick and 'Arry, with a couple of bob and a desperate urge to be noticed 'ad to 'ave one. Like now! Like yesterday!

My canny accountant 'ad anticipated this possibility. So there was 'is little SLK waiting to be owned and loved, while a 'uge waiting list was lengthening daily. Back to the old one-two. Not enough supply to meet demand.

So 'e found a dealer who was desperate for one of these new cars and said 'e could 'ave 'is... at a price. My accountant turned up at the showroom with 'is new-found dealer friend and let the dealer buy the car instead of 'im. The dealer 'anded over the money to the showroom, and paid my friend £7,000 pounds for letting 'im take 'is place in the waiting list.

This meant that even if you took away my accountant's £2,000 pound outlay 'e still made a profit of £5,000 pounds. In short, 'e'd got a result, and by all accounts so did the dealer who sold the car that afternoon to another customer for a profit of £3,000.

It was a bit of old fashioned 'orse trading, the likes of which goes on every day. What my mate the accountant did was to buy an option on 'is car, just like the boys in the City when they buy and sell derivatives. It's the same thing really, without the complicated language and the silly jackets.

Nice little wheeze though, isn't it? It's worth burying your 'ead in Motor Weekly or something just to get 'ot news of motor designs fresh off the drawing board.

LET YOUR FINGERS DO THE WORKING

Financial derivatives are bought and sold on a market known as LIFFE – the London International Financial Futures Exchange. It's a cacophony of chaos and clutter, everyone screaming and shouting, trying to buy and sell while standing in small rings known as pits. All the traders wear different brightly coloured jackets so they can recognise which company or bank they represent. Because no one can hear very well, the traders have a sign language. Should you ever feel the need to pop into LIFFE here's our little hands-on guide to what all their finger and hand waving means.

BUYING

A trader wishing to buy indicates this by turning the palm of the hand towards the body and away from the potential seller.

PRICING

Prices are conveyed by hand signals in front of the body. Fingers held vertically indicate the number 1 to 5, horizontal fingers represent 6 to 9. A clenched fist represents 0 or 10.

QUANTITY

Quantity signals are shown by using the same fingers and numeric codes as for prices, but units are registered on the chin and tens on the forehead

SELLING

A trader wishing to sell indicates this by turning the palm of the hand away from the body and towards and potential buyer.

EXPLAIN LORRAINE

'Owever painful this was for you to read, spare a thought for 'ow painful it was to write. But at least I now understand what these things are about. Let's 'ope you do too. Anyway, 'ere's a summary of the main points just in case you need reminding, or your brain's started leaking out your ears.

WORD IN YOUR EAR: Not the sort of investments for those with a dicky ticker.

The chapter in a nut shell

- The main types of derivatives are futures and options.

- Futures commit you to buy at a fixed price in the future.

- Options offer the choice to buy at fixed price in the future.

- These can be very risky forms of investment, with large profits and large losses being made.

CHAPTER 12

Playing Safe

THE SAFETY SCHEMES WHICH HELP MAKE YOUR SAVINGS SECURE

REASONS TO BE CAREFUL

Rules: One, Two, Three

1 The person who's got your best interests at heart is you. Financial advisers who work off a commission may be completely honest and impartial but they still make money when you decide to invest. So make sure you're happy about the advice before you take it.

2 Numbers are numbing – and if you hear too many interest rate quotes, expected capital returns or investment schemes, it's all too easy to get confused.

3 Money is hard to earn and easily lost. You made all the effort to make your money so don't jump to hasty decisions about where or with whom to entrust it.

So you've got to be careful, but that's easier said than done when you may not know as much as your financial adviser. Thousands of people have been sold pensions which just weren't right for them. Yet many of the salesmen and women were perfectly honest and many of the buyers were perfectly intelligent – so how come so many people got it so wrong?

Part of the reason is that they were bamboozled by the magic. Finance can be confusing and if it sounds good and is told to you by a nice bloke, the temptation is to think that all is well.

The truth is that investments are very down to earth. Of course there is some complex small print, but what you must do is ask simple questions. Investing is about protecting your money and making more of it, so there are some very simple things you need to know before making your investment choice. Getting the answers to these simple questions will save you a lot of trouble. It's not a foolproof system but it will provide you with an awful lot of help in making sure you come out with the products best suited for you.

Questions To Ask Yourself

1 Why do I want to invest? Is it to get a steady income, with a little coming in each month? Or do I prefer to build up the basic investment value so that when I cash it in, I have a larger lump sum to play with? Am I most concerned with protecting the real value of my savings and not too worried about making them grow more than the rate of inflation?

2 How long am I going to tie up my money for? If you cash-in investments early, you can lose money. Some investments only make sense if you're willing to leave them in for a substantial period of time.

3 Do I want to gamble with my money and what can I afford to lose? Anything and everything which doesn't offer a fixed and guaranteed rate of return is a gamble. Some gambles are riskier than others but just because an investment scheme is tax-free or popular, it doesn't mean it is risk free. PEPs or Personal Equity Plans are no more than stockmarket investments, and as we always hear, the price of shares can go down as well as up.

So once you've decided to get up from the armchair, turn off the TV and drag your money out of the bank to put into some other investment, it's time to think of some questions for the salespeople and advisers.

Questions To Ask Them

1 Can I lose money?

2 If I buy this investment, what do you get out of it in terms of commission etc?

3 Exactly how much better is this investment than the one I have now?

4 How long does my money have to be tied up for?

5 What would I lose if I needed to get hold of my money quickly or before the investment matures?

6 What happens if I stop paying into the investment – am I penalised or do I lose out anyway?

INVESTOR PROTECTION

The investment world is regulated and policed, which is all very reassuring. But however good the police force, it's still better not to get burgled in the first place. If you want to protect yourself against fraud, mis-selling or just bad advice, do like the Boy Scouts do and Be Prepared. Don't walk blindly into the arms of a financial salesman or adviser. Instead, go knowing what it is you want from your discussions.

Even if you're not clear about which products you want, be sure of your aim. Do you want to safeguard your money, risk it all in the hope of winning a fortune, provide yourself with a steady income or do you want capital growth?

If your investment loses value, there is little you can do but put it down to experience. However, under certain circumstances there are safety nets which will refund part or all of your investment. If you lose money because the UK investment firm has gone out of business or has defrauded its customers, then you may get part or all of your money back, as long as the firm has been listed on the Central Register.

Anyone in the UK who offers investment advice or takes your money to invest on your behalf, must be listed on the Central Register. It's easy to check whether they are listed. All you have to do is call the Central Register telephone number. The people at the other end of the phone will tell you whether the firm or person is properly registered and whether they are allowed to accept money to invest on your behalf.

The official Central Register can be contacted by calling: 0171 929 3652. You pay the normal cost of a telephone call, but the service is free. Details about who is on the

Central Register can also be found on the New Prestel computer service which you may find in large public libraries and Citizen Advice Bureaux.

To help those in real trouble, there is an Investors' Compensation Scheme. It has paid out over £100 million since it was started in 1988. The money is collected by a levy on all authorised investment firms. If a company or person, listed on the Central Register, cannot return a client's money, the Compensation Scheme authorities can declare the firm 'in default.' Once this has been done, investors can apply to the scheme for compensation. If a compensation plan is approved, the Investors Compensation Scheme will pay the first £30,000 of a claim in full and 90% of the next £20,000. That means the maximum payout is £48,000. The scheme covers all official investments such as stocks and shares, unit trusts, futures and options, personal pensions. If you are in any doubt about whether your investment is covered by the scheme call or write to:

Investors Compensation Scheme Ltd.,
Gavrelle House,
2-14 Bunhill Row,
London EC1Y 8RA
Tel: (0171) 628 8820

DEPOSIT PROTECTION SCHEME

The Deposit Protection Scheme is designed to safeguard the money you put in a bank by offering compensation for losses which are incurred as a result of the bank going bust.

Those banks which have been authorised by the Banking Act of 1987 and which are incorporated in the UK will be covered by the scheme. But if there is any doubt in your mind about whether the bank is part of the scheme, you can ask the bank itself or contact the Deposit Protection Board which will be able to advise you.

However, even if a bank is part of the scheme, it does not mean all of your deposits are completely guaranteed. Usually the scheme will only cover 90% of your deposits, up to a maximum payment of £18,000. The compensation levels may vary if you have made your deposit with a UK bank in another country.

If you are making deposits in a foreign country but in a bank which is part of the scheme, it is wise to be extra careful. Check how much compensation you would receive and whether the currency in which you have made your deposit is covered by the scheme. The only deposits which are covered are those made in ECUs and the currencies of the following countries: Austria, Belgium, Denmark, Finland, France, Germany, Greece, Iceland, Ireland, Italy, Luxembourg, Netherlands, Norway, Portugal, Spain, Sweden, United Kingdom.

Deposits made in banks in the Channel Islands and the Isle of Man are not part of the Deposit Protection Scheme.

As details and legislation surrounding the scheme may change, it is advisable to contact the banks for up-to-date information regarding the protection of your bank deposits.

All banks covered by the scheme will be able to give you a leaflet explaining the details of the protection offered.

BUILDING SOCIETY INVESTOR PROTECTION SCHEME

The Building Society Association boasts of an "outstanding record for safety". It says that for more than 50 years it has had an unblemished record and that no ordinary investor in a building society has ever lost any savings.

Part of the reason for this is that building societies are very restricted in how they can use depositors funds. A very large proportion of the funds must be used for the provision of mortgages secured on properties on which a valuation has been made. Those funds which aren't invested in this manner are mainly kept in authorised banks and government guaranteed securities.

However, if a building society, which is a member of the Investor Protection Scheme, was to get into financial difficulties, its depositors would to a large degree be protected against major financial loss.

The Investor Protection Scheme reimburses up to 90% of the amount placed in most types of share and deposit accounts, up to a value of £20,000, or the equivalent of 22,222 ECU – which ever is more. For joint accounts the level of protection applies to each named account holder, so it is effectively doubled to 90%, up to a value of £40,000 or 44,444 ECU (again, whichever is more).

A list of all of the societies covered by the scheme can be obtained from:

The Building Societies Association,
3 Savile Row,
London W1X 1AF
Tel: (0171) 440 2218

EXPLAIN LORRAINE

I've always liked seeing the Bobby on the beat. It gives you confidence, don't it? It rarely stops your 'ouse being robbed or your car being nicked, but knowing there's someone to turn to, someone who will try and get at least some of your stuff back and offer a shoulder to cry on, makes the whole experience a little more comforting. 'Aving the police nearby doesn't stop you taking precautions by double locking the doors and the like, it just gives you that 'feel good factor'.

Well I reckon the same goes for investments. 'Aving people to fall back on, preferably part of the establishment, doesn't mean that you shouldn't take great care. But it is nice to know you're not alone.

The chapter in a nut shell

If a bank or building society goes bust and they are part of the official compensation scheme, you should get part of your money back.

Generally 90% of your deposits will be returned. However, the building society will pay a maximum of £20,000 and the bank scheme will pay maximum of £18,000. There are exemptions, so check the details before depositing money.

Anyone taking deposits or offering advice should be listed on the Central Register. If a company is listed on the register and declared 'in default', some compensation may be paid to the investors. The Central Register can be contacted on 0171 929 3652

Investments are defined by the Financial Services Act. 'Investing' in ostriches, champagne, or gemstones is not defined as an official investment and therefore there is no safety net provided by the Investor Protection Scheme.

CHAPTER 13
The Product Pack

Adam! What I think would be dead fab wicked is if you could cobble together in your fabulously efficient way, a list of different saving accounts and investments, with a quick ready reckoning system of risk, benefits and who they're aimed at.

Then I could 'ave a butchers at them, peruse them at my leisure and make out my investment shopping list. That way I would be able to see where I was going as far as my finances were concerned. Then if I chose to visit an adviser, I could take my list along and show that I 'ad done my homework and that I 'ad an idea of which direction I wished to take. I could also use it as a reference to check any suggestions that an adviser might make.

Symbols would 'elp, I'm sure. 'Ow about some saucy little icons? That way it would make the whole thing more fun and I wouldn't forget them in a hurry.

So come on Adam. 'Ow about it?

THE KEY

 The return comes in the form of either variable or fixed interest rate but either way, except in extreme circumstances, there is little or no practical risk to your capital. The major concern is that the real value of your savings will fall as the interest paid either doesn't keep up with inflation or is low compared with other available investments.

 There is a risk to capital, so if your investment does badly you may get back less than you put in.

 The more bikers the greater the risk of losing capital.

ALTERNATIVE INVESTMENT MARKET (AIM)

Risk:

Description:

Companies listed on the Alternative Investment Market are generally not as large or well known as the companies with an official London Stock Exchange listing. Many of them are relatively new companies and as such do not have the proven track record of the fully quoted companies.

Suitable For:

Those with a bit of stockmarket experience who are looking to buy into a company which has substantial growth potential. AIM investors are often looking for capital growth as opposed to dividend income.

Tax Implications:

Dividends are paid after the basic rate of tax has been deducted. The tax can be reclaimed by non-taxpayers, but higher rate taxpayers will have to pay more. Any profits made by the sale of shares may be liable for capital gains tax.

Risk:

Because many AIM shares are issued by companies which are relatively new or have reached a new stage in their development, predicting the future is particularly difficult. Companies may develop new markets or carve out a significant chunk of established markets and thereby create wealth for themselves and their investors. Equally the new ventures may fail, leaving their share, with little or no value.

Fortune Rating:

When the stockmarket is booming or companies make major advances, share prices can rise dramatically. The reverse is also true and prices can fall as quickly and abruptly as they rose.

How To Buy:

Shares are bought through stock brokers. AIM shares can be included in a PEP although it is usually best to take advice before investing in AIM shares.

BANK (CURRENT) ACCOUNT

Risk:

Description:

There are a variety of current accounts on which you can write cheques. Many of the banks now offer interest-bearing current accounts, which pay small rates of interest and allow you immediate access to your money. This is not really an investment or a savings product and should be used only as a temporary place to store money to which you need quick access. If you usually have a lot of money sitting in your current account, you should think of looking for somewhere else which offers better rates of interest.

Suitable For:

Day-to-day money management.

Tax Implications:

Tax is already deducted from the interest paid on deposits. Tax is deducted at the lower rate. Higher rate taxpayers must pay the extra tax themselves. If you are a non-taxpayer you can apply to have the interest paid without any deductions. Ask the bank for details, you need form R85. If you forget or fail to do this, you can claim the tax back from the Inland Revenue.

Risk:

Make sure the bank is covered by the Bank Deposit Protection Scheme which can refund part of any losses due to a bank's collapse.

Fortune Rating:

There's no chance of making a fortune by keeping your savings in this type of account.

How To Buy:

Walk into any bank which is convenient for you and they will be happy to tell you how to open an account. You will need identification before they will open the account, so check with the bank which types of ID it requires.

BANK (DEPOSIT) ACCOUNT

Risk:

Description:

Cheques cannot be drawn on these accounts but the interest rate offered should be higher than that paid on a current account. There are few simple deposit accounts left, they now have flash names like Premium Reserve, Prime or Instant Savings Accounts. The interest rate often varies with the value of the deposit and how much notice you are prepared to give before withdrawing your money.

Rates change frequently but the BBC's text service, Ceefax, publishes a good guide to what's on offer. If you have a television capable of tuning into Ceefax, see pages 250 & 255 on BBC 2. Channel 4's text service has some rates on page 546.

Suitable For:

Those with lump sums to invest or those who have extra cash and need access to it between 1-90 days.

Tax Implications:

Income tax is deducted from the interest at the lower rate. Higher rate tax payers must pay the additional tax themselves. Non-taxpayers should apply to the bank to have their interest paid without any tax deductions ask for form R85.

Risk:

Make sure the bank is covered by the Bank Deposit Protection Scheme which can refund part of any losses due to a bank's collapse.

Fortune Rating:

The less likely you are to need quick access to your money, the more you will earn in interest.

How To Buy:

Walk into or write to any bank you chose and they will be more than happy to open an account for you. Check the rates of interest and the convenience of local branches before deciding on which bank you want.

CORPORATE BONDS

Risk:

Description:

A loan to a company which should be paid back at the end of the loan period. Interest is paid by the company at a fixed rate. Before the loan is paid back, bond holders can sell their bonds through stockbrokers. Although the interest rate is fixed, the bond's selling price is variable and changes according to the demand and supply.

Suitable For:

Those looking for a speculative investment which can provide capital growth and income.

Tax Implications:

There is no capital gains tax to pay although income tax must be paid on any interest payments.

Risk:

The risk of not having the loan repaid can be very real. It is important that you make sure you are comfortable with the credit worthiness of the company before buying one of its corporate bonds. Even if interest payments are made on time, there is the risk that the market price of the bond can fall.

Fortune Rating:

Bond prices can rise and fall. However if you hope to make massive profits from a bet that the company will boom, it may be better to consider buying its shares. The best that can happen to a bond is that it will eventually be repaid. A share can keep on growing in value as the company itself grows.

How To Buy:

Corporate bonds can be bought through brokers. You can also invest in bonds indirectly by purchasing some unit trusts or PEPs.

FUTURES & OPTIONS

Risk:

Description:

A futures contract commits the purchaser to buying something at a fixed price in the future. The agreement lasts for a specific period of time. Futures can be bought for commodities, shares, interest rates, and financial indices. An options contract provides you with the opportunity to buy at a fixed price in the future, but does not oblige you to buy. Just as with futures contracts, an options contract also lasts for a specific period of time.

Suitable For:

Speculative investors who like the thrill of a gamble or those with complex investment portfolios who want to hedge their investment strategies.

Tax Implications:

Subject to income and capital gains tax.

Risk:

While futures and options can be used to reduce risk, the extreme volatility of these markets can make the investment exceptionally risky.

Fortune Rating:

Along with the risk comes the opportunity for huge rewards and if you're willing to take a gamble and you're lucky, futures and options trading can bring you a fortune. If you're unlucky or unwise, they can also bring financial catastrophe.

How To Buy:

Through your stockbroker.

GILTS AND GOVERNMENT STOCK

Risk:

Description:

Government stock, gilt edged securities and gilts, are one and the same thing. The government borrows money by promising to pay the lender a fixed rate of interest over a set period of time. If you buy government stock for £100, you are in effect lending the £100 to the government. In return they will pay you interest on the loan and at the end of the fixed period, they will pay back the original sun they borrowed.

If you want the money returned before the fixed period has past, you can sell the gilts to someone else. Be aware though, that you may have to sell the gilts for less than you paid.

Suitable For:

Those who want a fixed rate of interest who are looking for the reliability of a government backed investment.

Tax Implications:

The lower rate of tax is deducted from the interest payments, although higher rate tax payers must pay more. Gilts are exempt from capital gains tax.

Risk:

They are called gilt-edged because the promise to pay the loan back, comes from the government and is therefore thought to be as safe as possible. However gilt investors risk a fall in the price of the stock and because the interest rate is fixed, long term gilt investors may find the interest rates being paid on the loan, fall short of the rates available elsewhere.

Fortune Rating:

Not just a steady income there is also the hope that you can make capital gains.

How To Buy:

Through a stock broker, bank or Post Office.

GOLD

Risk:

Description:

You can invest in gold jewellery, gold bars or gold coins. And if the lure of gold is too much to resist but you don't want to have the yellow metal itself, you can always invest in shares in gold mining companies.

Suitable For:

In the past gold was always thought of as an investment for troubled times. It was the international currency of the world. In times of revolution, political uncertainty or stockmarket collapse, you could put your gold in your pocket, walk out the country and buy a nice home somewhere far away. To a large extent people do not see gold investments quite like they used to and even in times of great financial turbulence, the gold price has not risen to the same extent as it would have in the past. However, to some people, it still offers the advantage of being a store of wealth which it is relatively easy to move about.

Tax Implications:

One of the biggest problems with buying gold coins and gold bars is that you usually have to pay VAT when you buy them, and you do not get it back when you sell them. Because of this, you have to sell at a price 17.5% more expensive than you bought, just to break even.

Risk:

The gold price has not performed well. In addition while your money is tied up in gold, it may look pretty but it's not earning any interest.

Fortune Rating:

There is little evidence that in the recent past, gold has been a great money spinner. Buy it if you want a gold necklace, a ring or gold coins, but not if you think it's going to make you a fortune. Of course, so called gold shares (in gold mining companies) are like other shares in that they can make large profits and losses.

How To Buy:

Through a member of the London Bullion Market Association. Or through coin dealers like Spinks.

INVESTMENT TRUSTS

Risk:

Description:

Investment trusts are companies which don't make anything or offer any service to the general public. They are entirely devoted to investing in other companies. They enable the small investor to spread their risk very widely but the difference between the unit trusts and the investment trust is that investment trusts are quoted on the stockmarket and the value of their shares varies according to market conditions. Usually the value of a trust's portfolio is lower than the total value of all its shares.

A dividend is usually paid once or twice a year and the shares in the investment trust can be sold on the stockmarket.

Suitable For:

Because the underlying investment is spread over a number of different shares, this is an appealing means for the small investor to spread their risk. They can be used either as a means of investing regular small sums or investing lump sums.

Tax Implications:

The dividend is paid after having had the lower rate of income tax deducted. Non-taxpayers can reclaim this amount but as ever, higher tax payers must pay the additional tax. Profits made by the sale of investment trust shares may be liable for capital gains tax.

Risk:

Because they are quoted on the stockmarket, the value of your shares can fall as well as rise. Your dividend payment is dependent on the performance of the investment trust.

Fortune Rating:

Like all stockmarket based investments your return is dependent on the performance of share prices. During a bull run, investment trusts can offer substantial rewards.

How To Buy:

Through a stockbroker.

NATIONAL SAVINGS 10th ISSUE (INDEX LINKED)

Risk:

Description:

This is an index-linked savings scheme, meaning that it is guaranteed to keep pace with inflation over the five year investment period. In fact these certificates will more than keep their value, as they pay a small rate above inflation.

Suitable For:

Those who want to be certain that whatever happens, their savings won't actually lose any spending power. Good for savers with either a lump sum or regular cash to invest who can keep their money locked away for five years.

Tax Implications:

There is no income tax or capital gains tax to pay on this investment and the details do not have to be specified on your tax return.

Risk:

This is a government run savings/investment scheme and you are guaranteed to get at least the rate of inflation added to your savings – so the risk factor is as small as can be. As long as you hold it for one year there is no penalty for early withdrawal, although because the higher rates of interest are paid near the end of the term, you may miss out on a substantial part of the interest payment. Re-invested certificates can be withdrawn after one month without penalty.

Fortune Rating:

This is no way to make a fortune. The Index Linked Saving Certificates are designed for safety and peace of mind rather than risk and reward. If you want to sleep peacefully at night and be sure your money is safe, this is for you. If you want to dream of riches and don't mind gambling to get them, then it's probably worth looking elsewhere.

How To Buy:

Available from Post Offices. Ask for leaflet DNS 763/96/02 or if that doesn't roll easily off the tongue just ask for the National Savings leaflet. More information can also be obtained by writing to: Saving Certificates, National Savings, Durham DH99 1NS. Tel: (0191) 386 4900

NATIONAL SAVINGS 44th ISSUE

Risk:

Description:

These offer a fixed rate of interest guaranteed for five years from the date of purchase. Even if the rate of interest offered by banks and building societies increases over that five year period, the rate paid on these Saving Certificates will remain fixed.

Suitable For:

Lump sum or regular savings can be invested. They are good for those who are prepared to keep money locked away for five years. Can be bought by anyone over seven years old, or it can be bought by someone else in the holder's name if the holder is under seven.

Tax Implications:

National Savings, Savings Certificates – 44th Issue are free of income tax and capital gains tax.

Risk:

Since they are backed by the government the risk of losing your invested sum is as small as small can be. However, if inflation rises above the fixed rate of interest paid on the certificates, the real spending power of your savings will fall. There is no penalty for early withdrawal but the certificates won't earn interest until after the first year. Re-invested certificates earn interest after one month.

Fortune Rating:

If inflation and interest rates fall over the five year investment period, these bonds may perform very well. However they are designed for those who are more concerned with the safety of their investment than the possibility of making a fortune.

How To Buy:

Available from Post Offices. Ask for leaflet number DNS 762/96/02 or the National Savings Certificates Leaflet. More information is available from: Savings Certificates, National Savings, Durham DH99 1NS. Tel: (0191) 386 4900

NATIONAL SAVINGS CAPITAL BONDS

Risk:

Description:

A guaranteed and fixed rate of interest is paid as long as the bonds are held for five years. Because the interest is paid gross, that is without tax being deducted, the investment can grow at a quicker rate than would otherwise be possible.

Suitable For:

Those willing to lock up savings for five years and happy to take the risk that interest rates and inflation will not be higher than the fixed rate on offer by the capital bonds.

Tax Implications:

Although these are not tax-free, interest is paid gross and it is up to the holder to pay the tax and declare it on their tax return.

Risk:

This is a government-backed scheme and the main risk is that over the five year investment period you may have been able to get a better return elsewhere, if interest rates are higher than you first predicted. There is no guarantee that the rate of return will keep pace with inflation. No interest is paid if the bonds are cashed-in during the first year.

Fortune Rating:

You know exactly what you're getting when you sign on the dotted line and as there's little risk involved there is also a limited reward. This is no quick way to fame and fortune.

How To Buy:

Available through the Post Office, ask for leaflet DNS 770/96/02 or the capital bonds brochure. Further details available from: Capital Bonds, National Savings, Glasgow G58 1SB Tel: (0141) 636 2602

NATIONAL SAVINGS CHILDREN'S BONUS BONDS – ISSUE H

Risk:

Description:

These can be bought by anyone over 16 years of age for anyone under 16 years of age. They offer a fixed rate of interest which is guaranteed as long as the bonds are held for five years. The bonds stop paying returns after the holder has reached the age of 21.

Suitable For:

Anyone under the age of 16 on the date of purchase. Possible alternative to woolly jumpers and socks as a birthday present from relatives.

Tax Implications:

Free of UK income tax and capital gains tax.

Risk:

This is a government-backed scheme and you are guaranteed a fixed rate of interest as long as you keep the certificates for five years. The biggest risk is that inflation and interest rates will be higher than the fixed rate offered by the children's bonus bonds.

If you cash them in early, you will lose a substantial amount of the interest, but what interest you have been paid is still tax free.

Fortune Rating:

Not a thrills and spills package but a steady savings scheme.

How To Buy:

Available from the Post Office, ask for leaflet DNS 769/96/02 or just the Children's Bonus Bonds Information. For more details contact: Children's Bonus Bonds, National Savings, Glasgow G5B 1SB Tel: (0141) 636 2602

NATIONAL SAVINGS
FIRST OPTION BONDS

Risk:

Description:

FIRST stands for Fixed Interest Rate Savings Tax-Paid. The interest rate is fixed and guaranteed for one year from the date of purchase. Every 12 months the saver can decide to commit themselves to another year in the scheme or cash-in the bonds at that stage. Ten days before the bond expires you should receive a letter offering you terms at which the bond can be extended or re-invested.

Suitable For:

Really designed for tax payers who want to be sure of a fixed rate of return on their savings and investments.

Tax Implications:

The lower rate of income tax is deducted at source. Higher rate tax payers must more.

Risk:

This is a government-backed scheme and the greatest risk is that inflation or interest rates will be higher than the fixed rate of return. If you liquidate the investment before the first year has finished you will receive no interest payment. After the first anniversary, you can withdraw your money early, but there are interest rate penalties to be paid.

Fortune Rating:

A fixed rate of return, so this is for the steady investor not for those who want to risk all and reap the reward.

How To Buy:

Information is available from the Post Office, ask for leaflet DNS 770/96/02 or the First Options Bond Leaflet. Further details available from: First Option Bonds, National Savings, Glasgow G58 1SB. Tel: (0141) 636 2602

NATIONAL SAVINGS INCOME BONDS

Risk:

Description:

This provides a monthly flow of income into your bank account or building society. The interest rates are not fixed, and not only vary over time but rise as the amount you deposit increases.

Suitable For:

Those with a lump sum to invest, in need of a monthly income and who wish their income to depend on a variable rate of interest. Can be very useful for non-tax payers.

Tax Implications:

Income bonds are not tax-free but the interest rate is paid without any tax being deducted at source. Tax payers must declare the interest in their tax return and pay the tax which is due.

Risk:

This is a government-backed scheme but because the income is dependent on a variable rate of interest, a fall in the level of interest rates will reduce your income flow.

Fortune Rating:

High rates of interest will obviously mean you get richer and richer so your chances of fame and fortune are higher than with the fixed interest rate schemes.

How To Buy:

Available through Post Office. More information can be obtained by writing to National Savings, Blackpool FY3 9YP. Telephone: (0645) 645000

NATIONAL SAVINGS INVESTMENT ACCOUNT

Risk:

Description:

A variable interest rate account is similar to a building society or bank deposit account although interest rates change less frequently than in banks or building societies. As a result if interest rates are rising, investment accounts may pay less than the average. However if interest rates are falling investment accounts may pay more than the average. The level of interest rate paid on deposits rises as the amount of money deposited increases.

Suitable For:

One months' notice is needed to withdraw money, although immediate access is possible if an interest rate penalty is paid. The investment account is therefore particularly suited to those who wish to save money in regular or irregular parcels. Because the money is not immediately accessible, this may be a good way of encouraging children to save. Children under seven cannot withdraw money from the account.

Tax Implications:

The interest earned on an investment account is is paid without tax being deducted. Tax payers are responsible for declaring the interest on their tax return and will have to pay the appropriate amount of tax.

Risk:

This is a government-backed scheme so there is no real risk to your capital. If you have to make an unexpected withdrawal and cannot afford to wait 30 days, you will pay an interest rate penalty.

Fortune Rating:

Of course it depends on what you put in, but don't expect this account to turn acorns into oaks overnight. There is no risk to speak of and therefore the reward is unlikely to be huge. More a product for the saving squirrels who want to put money away for rainy day.

How To Buy:

Available from Post Offices, ask for leaflet DNS 761/96/02 or more details available from Investment Account, National Savings, Glasgow G58 1SB. Tel: (0141) 649 4555

NATIONAL SAVINGS ORDINARY ACCOUNT

Risk:

Description:

The sister product to the investment account, although interest rate are lower and you have immediate access to your money. Interest rates are variable and they rise as the deposit value rises. There are restrictions on the amount you can withdraw each day, and you should be sure to check these restrictions meet your needs.

Suitable For:

Those who do not have a bank checking account and often use the Post Office, and so find it more convenient to withdraw and deposit money over a Post Office counter.

Tax Implications:

Interest is paid without tax being deducted. Tax payers should declare the interest on their tax return and pay the appropriate amount of tax. Although this is not a tax-free account, there is a small tax advantage in that no income tax is paid on the first £70 of interest each year or £140 if the account s held in two people's names.

Risk:

No risk to speak of to your capital, but you are fairly certain to get a poor rate of interest.

Fortune Rating:

About as low as you can go – more an account for convenience than giving any prospect of making real money.

How To Buy:

Ask for leaflet DNS 760/96/01 or for more details write to: Ordinary Account, National Savings, Glasgow G58 1SB. Tel: (0141) 649 4555

NATIONAL SAVINGS PENSIONERS BONDS

Risk:

Description:

The interest rate is fixed for five years and interest is paid monthly.

Suitable For:

A convenient method of generating a monthly income for pensioners. The capital is locked away for five years, so make sure you can do without the capital sum for that period of time.

Tax Implications:

The interest is paid without any tax deductions and tax payers must declare the interest on their tax return and pay the appropriate amount of tax.

Risk:

This is a government-backed scheme so there is no risk to speak of. Early withdrawal from the scheme will result in an interest rate penalty in which a penalty must be paid in exchange for quick access to the money.

Fortune Rating:

Not for high rollers, this is designed to provide a steady flow of income for those with capital sums to invest.

How To Buy:

Available from the Post Office ask for leaflet number DNS 768/96/02 or the pensioners bonds brochure. Further details available from: Pensioners gilts, National Savings, Blackpool FY3 9YP Tel: (01253) 766151

NATIONAL SAVINGS PREMIUM BONDS

Risk:

Description:

Not so much an investment, but a lottery ticket with go-faster stripes. Premium Bonds pay no interest but you can always get your money back with the added advantage that your ticket is entered for a monthly prize draw.

Suitable For:

Anyone who wants a bit of a gamble but doesn't want to risk their original stake.

Tax Implications:

Any winnings are free of tax – so it's doubles all round.

Risk:

The chances are that you won't be winning any prizes. Because Premium Bonds do not pay any interest, there is a high risk of your savings losing value since inflation will erode the face value of the bonds. However, because you can always get your stake back by cashing the premium bonds in, you will always be able to afford a bus home from the Post Office even if you don't get the opportunity to roll back in a Rolls Royce.

Fortune Rating:

The odds of winning any prize are 11,000 to one so you can make a fortune but you've got to be very fortunate.

How To Buy:

Available from the Post Office, ask for leaflet DNS 765/96/02 or for more details contact: Premium Bonds, National Savings, Blackpool FY3 9YP.

See page 106 for further details on Premium Bonds

OFEX

Risk:

Description:

OFEX is the smallest of the three equity markets and attracts many of the smallest companies. But there are also a number of household names listed, including National Parking Corporation, Arsenal Football Club and Shepherd Neame (the pubs and brewing group). The market is run by the London based brokers, JP Jenkins.

Suitable For:

Only for the wary. An OFEX investment is not for the uninitiated.

Tax Implications:

Dividends are paid after the basic rate of tax has been deducted. The tax can be reclaimed by non-taxpayers, but higher rate taxpayers will have to pay more.

Risk:

OFEX dealing is much riskier than on the other two stockmarkets. Part of the reason for this is because the market is small. There is not a great deal of trading in many shares and therefore you may find it difficult to sell when you want to, so you would be left holding the baby. OFEX companies also tend to be smaller and newer ventures with less of a proven track record. As a result, investments in OFEX can be a lot riskier.

Fortune Rating:

As with all stockmarket investments there is a heavy risk that share prices can fall suddenly. Since the companies quoted on OFEX are often smaller than those with a full London Stockmarket quotation, it may also be difficult to obtain information about a company and therefore difficult to make informed investment decisions.

How To Buy:

OFEX shares are bought through stockbrokers.

PEPS – Personal Equity Plans

Risk:

Description:

There are two types of basic PEP: general and single company, although there is in fact an amazing variety within these two broad categories, including: Corporate PEPS, unit trust PEPs and self-select PEPs. The principle behind all the different types of PEPs is the same. They all provide a tax-free way of investing in shares and a limited number of other securities. The fact that you have invested in a share through a PEP does NOT mean that you are protected from a fall in the price of the shares. This is a speculative investment, but it does offer the advantage of tax-free status which can be very appealing.

Suitable For:

PEPs advantages are most obvious for higher rate tax payers, because they save the most from the tax free status. However PEPs can be beneficial for all tax payers.

Tax Implications:

They are free of income tax and capital gains tax. However losses within a PEP cannot be written off against gains for tax purposes.

Risk:

Despite the fancy name, a PEP is a speculative investment which depends on the value of the stock. As we all know the value of shares can rise and fall at alarming rates and while many PEPs have offered very good rates of return, it is wise to remember that the money you have invested in a PEP is at risk.

Fortune Rating:

Although the value of your PEP can go down, it can also go up and in fact past experience shows that in the medium or longterm the stockmarket does perform well. This can be a place to make significant gains.

How To Buy:

PEPs are available through building societies, banks, stock brokers or directly from the PEP providers. There are loads of adverts for PEPS but a list of PEP providers can be obtained through PEPMA, which is the PEP Managers Association.

PERMANENT INTEREST BEARING SHARES (PIBS)

Risk:

Description:

Issued by building societies, PIBS are not shares in the normal sense of the word. They pay a fixed rate of interest and are traded on the stock exchange. Unlike bonds, there is no redemption date and the only way of getting your money back is to sell the PIBS to someone else. The price of the PIBS changes with market conditions.

Suitable For:

Generally used by those with some experience of the markets and with an existing investment portfolio. Because of the risk that the market price will fall, your capital is at risk and these should not be thought of as savings scheme.

Tax Implications:

The interest is paid net of the lower rate of tax and higher tax payers must pay additional tax. However there is no capital gains to pay on PIBS.

Risk:

The main risk is that the value of the PIBS will fall. PIBS are not included in the Building Society Saving Compensation scheme and PIBS investors are the last to be paid if the society is wound up.

Fortune Rating:

While you get a guaranteed interest payment, any chances you have of unexpected fame and fortune rest with the possibility that the market price of the PIBS will rise and you can therefore sell at a profit.

How To Buy:

PIBS are sold through stockbrokers.

SHARES

Risk:

Description:

Ordinary shares provide part ownership of the company from which the shares have been issued. As the owner of the share, you are entitled to some of the profit and a say in how the company should be run. Share prices are quoted on the stock exchange and can be found in the share listing pages of some of the national newspapers, like the *Financial Times*.

Suitable For:

Those looking for a speculative investment which can provide capital growth and income.

Tax Implications:

Dividends are paid after the basic rate of tax has been deducted. The tax can be reclaimed by non-taxpayers, but higher rate taxpayers will have to pay more. Any profits made by the sale of shares may be liable for Capital Gains Tax.

Risk:

There is always a risk that the price of your shares will fall. The level of the dividend pay out may also fall and dividends are often suspended if the company has financial problems or changes its dividend policy. The price of the shares is affected by many things and can fluctuate for reasons quite beyond the control of the company and its management.

Fortune Rating:

When the stockmarket is booming or companies make major advances, share prices can rise dramatically. The reverse is also true and prices can fall as quickly and abruptly as they rose.

How To Buy:

Shares can be bought through brokers. You can also invest in shares indirectly by purchasing unit trusts or PEPs. Although the major companies are given a full listing on the London Stock Exchange, shares can also be bought in companies with listings on the smaller exchanges: AIM and OFEX.

TESSA – TAX EXEMPT SPECIAL SAVINGS ACCOUNT

Risk:

Description:

A savings account in which the interest earnt is tax free, as long as the savings are left alone for five years.

There are lots of different types of TESSAs on offer, some of which provide a fixed rate of interest and some a variable or floating rate. Deciding which type to go for is a bit of gamble and depends on what you think will happen to interest rates over the next five years. Whatever type of TESSA you chose, the money saved in the schemes all benefits from not paying tax and TESSAs can therefore be a useful investment.

Suitable For:

A useful means of saving for a rainy day and as there are penalties for withdrawing the cash early, there are in-built incentives to save. A single lump sum can be invested or you can put money in your TESSA whenever you have some spare cash.

Tax Implications:

Hooray – No Tax To Pay. TESSAs are a tax free zone.

Risk:

TESSAs are provided by banks and building societies which are usually covered by compensation schemes if the institution goes bust. The main risk is not choosing the best performing TESSA, as you don't know what will happen to interest rates.

Fortune Rating:

This is not a very speculative scheme and although the returns can be very healthy they are not designed to astound. They are built to protect and suitable places for some of your longterm savings.

How To Buy:

There are many TESSA providers and the banks and building societies have a range of TESSAs on offer.

UNIT TRUSTS

Risk:

Description:

The biggest problem for small stockmarket investors is spreading their risk. It can be very dangerous to put all your money into one share as all it takes is one unexpected event or price movement to wipe out the whole stockmarket investment. However, if you only have a small amount of money to invest, it is impractical to try and spread that over a large number of shares. To overcome this problem, unit trusts and investment trusts were developed which pool resources from a large number of investors. In this way, even the small investor can buy a slice of a very diversified range of investments.

Unit trusts charge a management fee and the profits from investments are reduced by an according amount.

You make a profit when the value of your unit has increased. Units are bought back by the trust itself. Unit trust members also qualify for any distributions the trust makes through the year. These consist of the dividends accumulated by the trust from the shares it holds.

Suitable For:

Small investors and people who want to invest in the stockmarket but are not confident about picking specific shares. People who have limited funds to invest and want to spread their risk amongst a number of different shares.

Tax Implications:

Profits from the sale of units are liable for capital gains tax. The distributions are paid with the basic rate of tax deducted. Higher rate tax payers must pay additional tax and non-taxpayers can reclaim the tax paid.

Risk:

As with all shares, the value your investment may fall as well as rise. Unit trusts are allowed to have large spreads and therefore the difference between the buying and selling prices may be fairly big – which could disadvantage investors wanting to cash in their units.

When a trust buys units back from an investor, they will try and sell them on again to someone else. If they can't find anyone else to buy the units, they may have to sell some of their assets to pay the original investor back. For those still in the unit trust, it means the value of the investment pool has fallen. If investors lose confidence in unit trusts, they can lose value very quickly.

Fortune Rating:

Any losses are shared out amongst all the unit holders but then of course, so are the gains. Still, a large rise in the stockmarket will hopefully bring you some rich rewards. But be prepared to take some losses as well.

How To Buy:

You will see plenty of adverts for the various unit trusts on the market but it's wise to take a look at some of the performance tables. Some of these are published in magazines like *Money Management*. If you want further information abut the rules and regulations governing unit trusts, contact the Association of Unit Trusts and Investment Funds (AUTIF). Telephone: (0171) 831 0898.

FACT FILE
THE PREMIUM BOND

Harold MacMillan introduced the premium bond on 17th April 1956, when he was Chancellor of the Exchequer.

Today premium bonds come in £1 denominations but the minimum purchase is £100. Once you have bought into the scheme, each month you are entered into the prize draw which range from £50 – £1 million. Unlike the National Lottery where a ticket only gives you one chance of success, a premium bond buys you an unlimited number of goes in the national draw. And it's attractions like that which have persuaded about 23 million people to buy a bond. That's about half the UK population, in other words: a fleet of 12,333 full QE2s or 287 full Wembley Stadiums.

Even though they are popular, winning any of the large prizes is highly unlikely. If you want to be rich quick the good news is that there is a one million pound prize on offer every month and when you add all the smaller prizes together, there is over £35 million worth of prize money available each month. The bad news is that your chances of winning are not great. If you want to increase your chances, you have to buy more bonds.

PRIZE	ODDS OF WINNING
£1,000,000	1 in 8.9 billion
£100,000	1 in 1.78 billion
£10,000	1 in 181.56 million
£1,000	1 in 1.42 million
£500	1 in 1.4 million
£100	1 in 129,576
£50	1 in 22,757
£ ANY PRIZE	1 in 19,000

And if you can't sleep at night because you think that the poor old clerk who has to feed all the premium bond numbers into ERNIE may in his confusion have forgotten to put yours in, let me bring peace and tranquillity to your nighttime slumbers with this piece of information.

Your premium bond numbers have definitely not been entered into ERNIE!

That's because to avoid any mistakes the premium bond bosses decided not to feed anybody's numbers into ERNIE, so none could be left out by mistake. All ERNIE does is generate random numbers. If they coincide with the numbers on your premium bond – then you are a winner. Of course that always leaves the possibility that the computer which checks who has won may not be working – but then what would life be without a little worry?

SAY HELLO TO ERNIE

ERNIE is the computer which chooses the numbers of the winning premium bonds. Its name is really an acronym which stands for Electronic Random Number Indicator Equipment. ERNIE actually made his first appearance on 26th July 1956 and since then (although they carry the same name) there have been three computers picking the premium bond winners: ERNIE mark 1, mark 2 and mark 3.

Fascinating Facts About ERNIE and His Premium Bonds

There are £14 million worth of uncollected prizes.

Uncollected prizes will be held for the winner forever.

There are £8.9 billion worth of premium bonds in existence.

Each bond has an equal chance of winning.

Buying bonds in consecutive numbers has no effect on your chances of winning.

You can buy from £100 – £20,000 worth of bonds.

Anyone over the age of 16 can buy bonds.

Purchases above £100 are sold in multiples of £10.

Bonds can be bought for children under 16 by their great grandparents grandparents, parents or guardians.

You have to hold your bonds for one complete month after purchase before they are entered into the monthly draw.

If you have won a prize you will be sent a letter telling you how much you have won.

All winners' names are confidential. They are only released if the winner wants to publicise their winnings, otherwise their names are withheld.

Winning numbers are available at the Post Office, two months after the draw.

If you are moving address or believe you may have won something but have not been informed because you moved home since last giving your address to the premium bond office, write to:

> Premium Bonds,
> National Savings,
> Blackpool FY3 9YP

with a list of your premium bond numbers.

If you have lost your premium bond numbers, write to the above address with your full name, current/previous address and date of birth and they will supply you with a reminder of the numbers.

You can cash in all or part of your premium bond holdings and you will get back the face value of the bonds, which is the amount you originally paid for them. At the Post Office ask for the premium bond repayment form (DNS 303). You should get your cash back in just over one week.

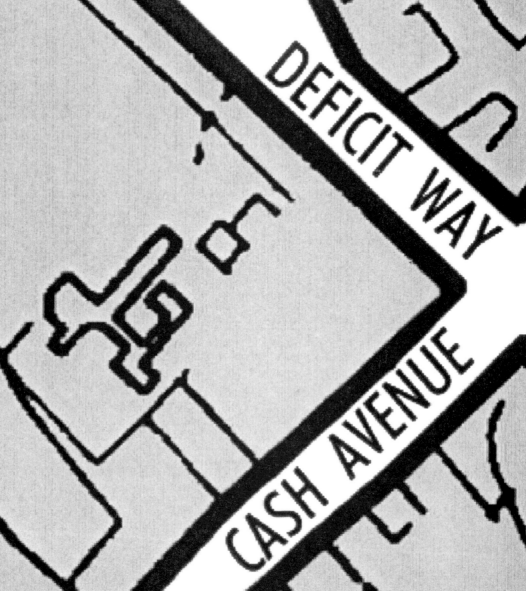

APPENDIX

The A-Z of Money

A GUIDE FOR THE PERPLEXED. 40 EASY TO UNDERSTAND PAGES OF DEFINITIONS AND EXPLANATIONS COVERING TERMS, CONCEPTS AND DOUBLE-TALK FROM THE WORLD OF MONEY.

Just a little story of an incident I can remember when I first started appearing on telly regularly. I was asked by a lovely geezer called Norman Newell, who was 'ead of EMI at the time, if I could sing. I auditioned for 'im with a song called 'Words'. Well 'e liked it and 'e ended up writing me a song which we duly recorded. We became great friends and one Christmas 'e invited me to a lunch party with a group of people, one of whom was a very pompous man from America.

During the whole lunch this American talked down to me, using very long words. At the time I used to carry a pocket dictionary with me, the reason being I got caught out on long words fairly regularly. Often if you asked the person using the word what it meant, they had no idea. Well anyway, I got into the 'abit of waiting for an appropriate moment to disappear to the toilet to look it up. Not easy when you're a lousy speller. I was determined not to be rude to this American but then 'e asked me my age. I was 27 years old at the time. "Really" 'e said "I thought you were

about 17" I though how nice and said so. To which he replied "Oh, mental age of course." Well that was it, as 'e seemed to think I was a twit anyway, the next time 'e said something I didn't understand, I asked what the word meant. Now as it 'appens no-one could agree on what the word meant. So I said "Ere, 'old on I'll look it up in my dictionary." A suitable gasp of surprise from everyone at the table. I suppose you could say we had entered into a kind of Call My Bluff. For goodness sake, who ever carries round a dictionary? In fact the old boy was wrong, he didn't even know what the word 'e was using meant.

"You know" I said, "you are very naughty. If you assumed my mental age was 17, why 'ave you continually spoken to me in long words? Surely the whole point of conversation is to converse, to be understood and not to make the other person feel small."

Anyway this book is a bit like a conversation and if there were any words you didn't understand in it, 'ere's your own personal dictionary to oik out when in doubt.

is for arbitrage

ACT
Nothing to do with what happens on the stage of the Royal Shakespeare Company, this stands for Advanced Corporation Tax.

Administration
A company that is going bankrupt may apply to the courts for administration. If granted, this would save the company from having to close down immediately. An administrator would be appointed to run the company and perhaps find a buyer for either parts of the company or for the whole venture.

ADR
American Depository Receipts – a package of shares designed for the American. An ADR is little more than a receipt which says that a certain amount of shares is being held by a bank in the company's home country. Dividends and taxes are collected and paid through the bank, although the dividends are then converted into dollars and paid to the ADR holder. Trading in ADRs as opposed to trading in the shares themselves saves the investor from paying stamp duty on each transaction. When a company creates its pool of ADRs the company pays an initial stamp duty which exempts investors from having to pay the tax each time the ADRs are traded.

After Hours Trading/Dealing
Buying or selling after the end of the official close of the market. Normal trading on the London Stock Exchange ends at 4.30pm but trades can still be registered until 5.15pm each weekday.

AIM
Otherwise known as the Alternative Investment Market. Requirements for floating on AIM are less stringent than those for

obtaining a full listing on the London Stock Exchange. AIM therefore provides an attractive way for small companies to obtain extra funds. (Also see OFEX)

Amortisation

The American term for depreciation.

Angel

A business angel is an investor, usually a successful businessman or woman, who not only offers investment finance but gives advice to new companies or business ventures. Angels are also the people who provide financial backing to theatrical productions.

Arbitrage

This is taking advantage of the difference in price of securities in two different markets. For example if *Chase Me* securities cost £5 in London but only £4.99 in Hong Kong, you could make a profit by buying the shares in Hong Kong and selling them immediately in London. The people who do this sort of business are called Arbitrageurs. Apart from lining their own pockets, Arbitrageurs can serve a useful purpose in regulating the market. For example, if *Chase Me* shares are cheaper in Hong Kong than elsewhere, the Arbitrageur will continue to buy them from the Hong Kong market until he drives the price up to the level at which there is no profit in buying them from Hong Kong. In this way the Arbitrageur helps in making sure prices for identical products are the same in all markets.

In reality their profit margins are wafer thin and to make the most of their profits, Arbitrageurs buy and sell in huge quantities.

Annual General Meeting (AGM)

Each year all public companies must hold a meeting at which any of its shareholders can gather. At the meeting the shareholders vote to accept or reject the company's accounts and decide whether to re-elect the directors. AGM's are not democratic, there is no one member, one vote rule. The amount of votes depends on the amount of shares you hold. For small shareholders the AGM is a public platform on which they have a larger chance of getting publicity for their complaints. However it is difficult for them to get their way as they only have a small proportion of the voting power.

Annuity

This provides the purchaser with a guaranteed income for life. When you retire, your pension fund is used to buy an annuity to provide you with your weekly or monthly income.

APR

Otherwise known as the Annualised Percentage Rate. This is the real cost of a loan or credit purchase. For the purposes of interest rate calculations, when you start making your monthly repayments on the money you owe on a higher purchase deal, the interest rate is calculated not on the remaining debt (the bits you haven't paid off yet) but on the whole debt. The APR will therefore be higher than the flat rate of interest.

Asset

A company's or person's possessions are known as their assets. Even trademarks or the more intangible concept of customer goodwill may be counted as an asset.

Asset Allocation

The process by which individuals or companies decide in which things to invest and how much they should invest in each choice.

Asset Stripping

This is usually used in a derogatory sense and means to buy a company because you want to dismantle it and sell off the separate parts.

This of course is very bad news for the workers in the company as it may result in them being made redundant. Asset Stripping can make financial sense for the person who has bought the company if the sum of the parts is worth more than the total value of the company. (See Unbundling)

At Best

An instruction to a broker to buy or sell at the best possible price. In the time that it takes to take an order and to carry it out, the sale or purchase price may change, so a client may tell a broker to trade at best, meaning they must get the most advantageous price possible even if it's not the one quoted on the phone.

Auditor's Report

An auditor's report is part of a company's accounts. The report says whether or not the accounts give a fair and true picture of the financial position of the company and that the whole thing is not a load of baloney.

Authorised Capital

This is the value of the shares a company is allowed to issue without further permission from shareholders.

AVCs

Additional Voluntary Contributions are used if the holder of a pension wishes to pay in larger amounts into their company pension fund.

LORRAINE'S ALTERNATIVE DEFINITIONS

ASSETS: What ladies on Page 3 have.

ASSET LOCATION: Where they have them.

ASSET STRIPING: What they do to show them off.

is for bears

Back Office
The department of a broking house where all the paperwork is done

Backwardation
A term used in the commodity market – where things like orange juice, wheat or pork bellies are traded – to describe the situation where the futures price is lower than the cash price.

Balance of Payments
The record of payments between one country and all its other foreign trading partners. When a British driver buys a German car, money flows out of Britain into Germany and this is counted as a debit on the balance of payments. If a German buys some British clothes, then money flows the other way out of Germany and into Britain and this is counted as a credit on the balance of payments. Therefore when people say a country is running a balance of payments deficit, they mean the country is importing more goods and services than it is exporting. When a country is said to be running a balance of payments surplus, it has been exporting more goods and services than it imported.

Balance Sheet
In some ways it's like a bank account statement for companies, which describes their financial position. But the balance sheet tells you much more than how much money a company has in its piggy bank. Amongst other details it provides are the value of the fixed assets, depreciation, investments, goods held in stock, the money it owes to others and the amount of money which is owed to the company.

BAMBI
A Bloody Awful Management Buy-In (See MBI)

Lorraines's Little Somethings

DID YOU KNOW that banking originated in Italy, where a group of Italian Merchants would sit on benches in a large hall and make all their fancy deals? If one of them reneged on a deal he was thrown out of the hall and his bench was broken. The Italian name for bench is Banco and the Italian for broken is Rupto – hence the saying – Bankrupt.

Basis Point

Used in the description of interest rate moves, one basis point is one hundredth of a percentage point. A 50 basis points rise in the interest rate means it has gone up by half of one percent.

Bear

An investor or commentator who thinks the market is about to fall is called a bear. Bearish news is news which will make the market fall, and a bear market is one which is already falling. Presumably bear markets fall in price because they're having the life squeezed from them in a bear-like hug. (See Bull)

Bearer Bonds

This is not registered in anyone's name but belongs to whoever has hold of it, rather like a five pound note.

Bed & Breakfast

No cups of tea, seaside views or peculiar landladies I'm afraid. This involves selling shares one night only to buy the same things back the next morning. It's a bit of daftness which is done for tax purposes.

You are allowed to make a certain amount of profit (capital gains) from your investments each year, before you are taxed. Unfortunately you can't just watch your profits grow year by year and when it suits you cash them in and expect not to pay tax. To avoid the tax man's grasp you have to realise the profit each tax year. As a result investors who wish to take advantage of the capital gains allowance, 'bed and breakfast' their shares: sell them and buy them back the next day. If you are thinking of bed and breakfasting the shares yourself, be aware that there are trading costs involved and that your particular circumstances may mean it is not necessary or wise for you to take advantage of this tax break. There is always the risk of course that overnight, the value of your shares will change, so there is a real trading risk involved. Think carefully or take advice before you get into this annual ritual.

Bellwether Stock

A share which is thought to be indicative of the market or economy as a whole. A fall in the price of a Bellwether Stock is therefore thought to give a clue as to the possible future direction of the whole stockmarket or can give a warning about problems building up in the economy.

Bid Price

This is the price at which a share investor or market maker is willing to buy.

Big Bang

The big date was 27th October 1986 and it marked the beginning of computer share trading on the London stockmarket and the disappearance of Open Outcry on the exchange floor. No more waving and shouting, now it's just people at desks and computers screens.

Big Board

The nickname of the New York Stock Exchange.

Black Economy

Sometimes known as the Shadow Economy. Whatever its name, it is the work and deals done on the sly and out of reach from the tax man.

Black Monday

On October 19th 1987, the Dow Jones Industrial Index of share prices fell over 508 points losing over 22% of its value in just one day. The loss led to a major fall on the London Stockmarket.

Black Knight

A person or company which launches a hostile takeover bid.

Blue Chip

In casino gambling the highest value betting chip is blue and so blue chip companies are those which are most highly valued and regarded.

Bond

The name's bond, gilt bond, long bond or corporate bond. In fact there is a whole family of bonds who have never driven a Lotus or been thrown from a moving train. Bonds are a way in which companies, governments or local authorities can borrow money. Instead of going to the bank the organisation sells a bond on the market, the buyer is entitled to a regular interest rate payment and at the end of an agreed period of time gets the original loan back.

Bottom Feeding

Nothing to do with biting behinds, bottom feeding actually means buying an investment when the price is low, or near the bottom of its range and hoping that it will then rise in price.

Break-even Point

The point at which a company or other financial venture just covers its costs and neither makes a profit or loss.

Broker

Brokers are members of the London Stock Exchange. They may offer advice to their clients on which shares to buy or sell and carry out the deals on the clients' behalf. Brokers may also buy and sell for themselves, when a broker deals in this manner, they are said to have dealt on their own account.

Before the changes in the market of 1986, known as Big Bang, brokers were not allowed to trade in shares and instead concentrated on advising clients. The actual buying and selling was left to the jobbers on the stock exchange floor. Today the distinction no longer exists and brokers can both advise and trade in shares.

Bull

An investor or commentator who thinks the market is about to rise is called a bull. Bullish news is news which will make the market rise, and a bull market is one which is already rising. (See Bear)

Business Plan

A detailed explanation of the plans of a new or expanding company and an explanation of how it intends to organise itself, conduct its business and most importantly, make money.

LORRAINE'S ALTERNATIVE DEFINITIONS

BIG BANG: *When the world was made.*

BACK OFFICE: *Where the dirty deals are dealt.*

BED & BREAKFAST: *Yuk, touring in a play.*

BUSINESS PLAN: *What I lack*

BOTTOM FEEDING: *Reverse colonic irrigation*

is for cash cow

Call Option
The right, but not the obligation, to buy shares or other financial instruments at an agreed price and date in the future.

Cash Cow
A product or company division which generates money and profit as reliably as a cow produces milk.

Cash Market
The market for immediate delivery as opposed to the futures market where you buy for future delivery.

Chartist
A financial analyst who predicts the future by analysing graph price patterns, many of the patterns are given daft names like 'Dead Cat Bounce' (see separate entry).

Chinese Walls
Since Big Bang the rules were changed to allow brokers to: advise clients on which shares to buy and sell; help companies raise money; and buy and sell shares on their own behalf. The rule change raised fears that a conflict of interest would arise. Because they had their fingers in so many pies, the brokers could have confidential information which they could exploit by selling or buying the right shares. To prevent this happening, metaphorical Chinese Walls were put in place. The walls are meant to separate the various divisions of a company and therefore keep the different divisions ignorant of each other's activities. In this way a single company should not be able to profit from their access to privileged and confidential information.

Commission
The fee which a broker charges his/her client for dealing on their behalf.

Commodity

In its widest sense it is used to describe any product which can be bought and sold, but it is more commonly used to describe the specific products traded on the various commodity exchanges. These products are of an agricultural, mined or natural nature, like wheat, rubber, coffee, orange juice and sugar.

Coupon

Very much like the '10 pence off a packet of washing powder' coupon you take to the supermarket. The difference is that financial coupons are often attached to bearer bonds and are exchanged for dividend payments.

The term coupon is also used to describe the rate at which interest is paid on the face value of a bond. A 10% coupon means the bond pays 10% of its face value each year. However, because the traded value can differ from the face value, the real interest rate can differ from the coupon interest rate. And if that explanation was as indigestible as a frozen TV dinner, try looking at our chapter on bonds, which will help it slide down the gullet as smoothly as a bottle of Bailey's.

Cum

A Latin word meaning 'with'. Most often seen as Cum dividend, meaning that the share buyer has the rights to the next scheduled dividend. Cum dividend is the opposite of Ex dividend which means the buyer no longer has the right to the next scheduled dividend.

Cyclical Stock

Shares which are particularly prone to being affected by a rise or fall in the general well-being of the economy.

LORRAINE'S ALTERNATIVE DEFINITIONS

CALL OPTION: *"Please hold the line .....*
the person on the phone knows you are
waiting ... Please hold the line .... the
person on the phone knows you are waiting."

CASH COW: *Ivana Trump?*

COMMISSION: *What my agent gets too much of.*

is for dawn raid

Dawn Raid

When a company launches a takeover attack just as the stockmarket opens for morning business.

Boy, do I know about them! Funny that. I never could understand why the coppers wanted to see my dad so early.

Dead Cat Bounce

The term used to describe a particular price pattern. The price falls sharply and then hardly bounces back at all. Dead cats don't bounce.

Dealer

A person who buys and sells securities.

Debenture

A corporate bond backed by the assets of the issuing company.

Depreciation

The process of reducing the value of assets in a company's accounts. The rate at which the value of an asset is reduced is important for the tax and profit position of any company.

Dividend

Part of a company's profits are paid to the shareholders as dividends. The value of the dividend payout varies according to the size of profits and the policy of the company. Dividends are often paid twice a year – once when the company reports its interim results and once when it publishes its full year results, although in some cases a company may withhold a dividend payment. A shareholder is charged income tax on their dividend payments as opposed to the capital gains tax. The dividend already has the basic rate of tax deducted and so there is no more tax to pay unless the shareholder pays above the basic rate of tax.

Dow Jones Industrial Index

The most often used measure of how well the New York stock exchange has been doing. It reflects the price movement of 30 of the top mainly industrial companies in the US. The Dow Jones was introduced in 1928. There are other measures of stockmarket performance which look at a wider range of companies, these include S&P 500 and the Nasdaq Composite.

Downgrade

Lowering the credit rating.

Downsizing

Reducing the size of the work-force. The word downsizing is often used because it sounds better than announcing mass layoffs.

LORRAINE'S ALTERNATIVE DEFINITIONS

DOWNSIZING: *The carrot juice diet.*

is for extraordinary general meeting

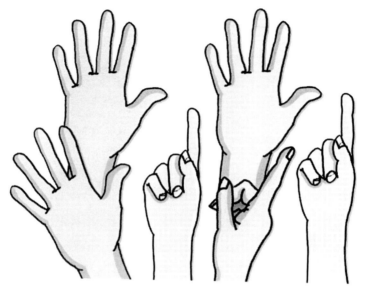

Earnings Per Share
A company's profits after tax divided by the number of ordinary shares it has issued.

ECU
Stands for the European Currency Unit. It's not quite a currency in the same sense as the pound, dollar or deutschmark, since you can't actually walk into a sweet shop and buy a packet of mints with it. It was created in 1978. Because you don't find ECUs folded in people's wallets or lying in their piggy banks, its main use is as a reference point for the European authorities making pan-European comparisons.

EGM
An Extraordinary General Meeting can be called by a company to discuss, and then either approve or reject, any unusual set of circumstances for which the board of management needs shareholder approval. An EGM would be called, for instance, to approve or reject a takeover bid.

Endowment Mortgages
A mortgage which has a life assurance policy as well. Holders of endowment mortgages pay the lender interest but do not pay off any of the money they originally borrowed. Instead the mortgage holder pays into a life assurance policy which, when it matures, will hopefully be able to pay off the original loan. However there is no guarantee that the life assurance policy will be able to pay off the mortgage, which means the mortgage holder would have to find the money from somewhere else. If the policy holder dies, the mortgage is paid off by the life policy element of the mortgage. Payment on the life policy is dependent on a number of restrictions and details should be checked before an agreement is entered into. If all goes well, the policy may have enough

not only to pay off the mortgage but to provide a lump sum with which the mortgage holder can fund their escape to the Caribbean, get that face-lift they always wanted or just fund a life of ease and eating out. In the past there has been some criticism that the risks associated with endowment mortgages have not been fully explained to customers.

Entrepreneur
The business men and women who take risks in setting up new financial ventures and survive on the profit they make.

ERM
The Exchange Rate Mechanism is a system which links some of Europe's currencies. The mechanism restricts the amount by which any one currency can fluctuate against the rest. Its purpose was, in part, to introduce more stability between European currency values.

Equity
Otherwise known as shares. A company's shareholders are its owners.

Eurobonds
A bond denominated in a currency different from that of the country in which the bond has been issued. So a British investor might buy a dollar bond and a German investor might buy a Yen bond. These are usually bearer bonds meaning that there is no record of who owns them.

Ex
Meaning "without". When a share goes ex-dividend it means from that date buyers of the share are not entitled to the forthcoming scheduled dividend pay-out. Buyers of the share will be entitled to the dividend from the moment it goes cum-dividend again.

Exchange Rate
Not all currencies are of the same value, so one dollar is not worth the same as one pound. The exchange rate tells you how much of one currency you need to buy a unit of another currency. So when they say the pound is trading against the German mark at 2.44, it means that for every one pound you can get 2.44 German marks.

Execution-only
An execution-only service is one in which the broker offers no advice as to the best course of action, but just carries out the orders of his/her client.

Exercise
Something most desk-bound investors, speculators and market professionals, don't do enough of. But it has another meaning apart from the one associated with brisk walks and lifting weights. If you have an option to buy shares and then decide to use the option, you are said to have exercised the option.

Expiry
A six months option to buy a share is said to have expired after the six months has elapsed.

LORRAINE'S ALTERNATIVE DEFINITIONS

ERM: What I say when people confuse me ...erm

EXERCISE: Breaking sweat

EXPIRY: What happens after exercise.

EX: Redundancy, as in matrimony.

is for FTSE

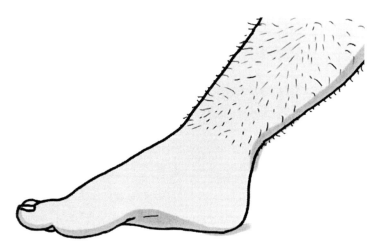

Federal Reserve
The US Central Bank.

Final Dividend
The dividend paid by a company at the end of its financial year.

Financial Advisers
These can be fee-based or paid on commission and it is wise to find out how they are paid before you take their advice. There are two main types of financial adviser: the tied agent and the independent. Tied agents usually act for one of the large insurance companies and can only sell that company's products. The independent adviser can offer a wide range of advice and sell most people's products. Independent advisers can be paid on a commission or fee basis. Some advisers give you the choice of how you would like to pay, but not all of them are so flexible and it is therefore advisable to check before booking an appointment.

Fiscal Year
The fiscal year is different from the calender year and runs from April 5th – April 4th and is otherwise known as the tax year. Your income and tax are judged over the fiscal year and not the calendar year.

Fixed Rate
An interest rate or exchange rate which is fixed and therefore does not move. This is the opposite of a floating rate which moves depending on market forces.

Flotation
When a company first offers its shares to the public, it is said to have floated.

Floating Rate
An interest rate or exchange rate which is not fixed, but is allowed to move depending on where market forces push it.

Flipper

A lovely dolphin star of a 1970's television series or a trader who holds stock for only a few days before he/she sells it to someone else.

Foreign Exchanges

The markets on which currencies are bought and sold.

FTSE Index

It stands for the Financial Times Stock Exchange Index. When people say the FTSE, they usually mean the FTSE 100 Index, which is the most widely used measure of performance for the London Stockmarket. It was first introduced on 31st December 1983 and reflects the movement of the top 100 most valuable companies on the stockmarket.

The FTSE family of indices are calculated and administered by a company half owned by the London Stock Exchange and half owned by the *Financial Times*.

In addition to the FTSE 100 Index there are other indices which reflect movements in the stockmarket, by looking at different groups of companies.

FTSE 250: *Reflects the movements in the shares of the next 250 most valuable companies not included in the FTSE 100 index. Value is determined by market capitalisation.*

FTSE 350: *Reflects the movement of the shares of the most valuable 350 companies.*

FTSE All-Share: *The index is designed to cover those companies which make up between 98-99% of the total stockmarket value. The calculation is checked each December. There are about 900 companies included in the index. The index was first introduced in 1962.*

FTSE Fledgling: *This includes all the shares not covered by the FTSE All-Share Index. As a percentage of the total value of the market this is very small, but the FTSE Fledgling Index still includes about 900 companies, which just goes to show there are an awful lot of small quoted companies out there.*

FTSE Small Cap: *Reflects the movement in the share price of the smaller quoted companies on the stockmarket. It was introduced on 31st December 1992.*

FTSE Eurotrack 100: *Reflects the price movement of an international range of major shares. The countries covered by the index are: Austria, Belgium, Finland, France, Germany, Ireland, Netherlands, Spain, Sweden, Switzerland, Norway, Denmark, Italy – all of which sounds like an announcement from the Eurovision Song contest. One country noticeable for its absence from that list is the UK. The FTSE Eurotrack 200, takes the Eurotrack 100 and adds the FTSE 100 to it. The Eurotrack 100 was introduced in October 1990 and the Eurotrack 200 was introduced in February 1991.*

And I thought Footsie was what you played under the table.

Fundamental Analysis

Fundamental and technical analysis are two ways of examining a share's value. Technical analysis examines a share by looking at the past graph patterns of its price and trading volume. Technical analysts hope to spot key patterns or trends which precede a key movement in the price. By spotting these trends, they hope to predict important share price movements. Fundamental analysis is the flip side of the coin. As its name suggests, it involves an examination of the fundamental building blocks on which the business is based, its earning potential and organisation.

Futures

A futures contract is an obligation to buy or sell a commodity or share at some fixed future date and at fixed price.

is for gemms

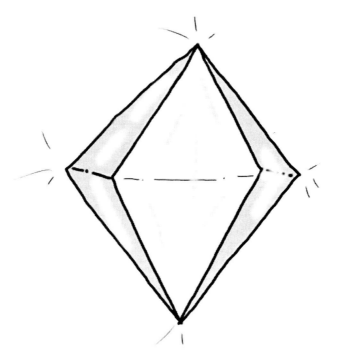

Gearing

Used to measure the amount of debt a company has in proportion to the value of all its shares put together. For example if the combined value of all its shares (market capitalisation) was £200 million and its net debt was £100 million, the company would have a gearing ratio of 50%.

GEMMs

Gilt-edged market makers or market makers who trade in gilt-edged securities – which ever you prefer.

Gilt Edged

The name given to bonds issued by the UK government. They are called gilt-edged

because the risk of the government failing to pay keep up the interest payments and eventually pay back the loan, is thought to be very small.

Golden Share

A share with very powerful voting rights. When the government privatised a number of previously state-owned companies, it often decided to keep hold of a golden share so it had some measure of control over the company.

Grey Market

Before a share is launched on the official stockmarket, some trading can still take place in what is known as the Grey Market. It is not a place nor a building and it's not run by any one company. The Grey Market is actually a shadowy sort of world in which people buy and sell shares before they have even been issued and allotted. Sellers therefore do not know how many shares they have to sell. Trading in the Grey Market can give a useful indication of what investors think the shares are worth before official trading begins.

Gross

The value of interest rates, dividends etc. before any deductions like income tax, have been made.

LORRAINE'S ALTERNATIVE DEFINITIONS

GEMMS: "Diamonds, Diamonds.. OOh Fab Diamonds."

GROSS: Ugh – revolting.

G: Spot

is for hockey stick

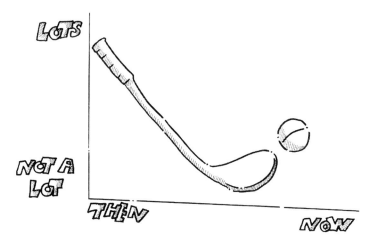

Head and Shoulders

Used to describe a performance pattern which resembles a very pointy outline of a head and shoulder.

Hedging

The process of trying to protect yourself through investment strategies.

A company which has to import from Germany and therefore buy deutchmarks to pay for the imports, may decide to hedge against the risk of a rise in the value of the deutschmark. It would do this by buying the currency on the futures market or buying an option on the currency. In this way it knows the amount it has to pay for its deutschmarks and therefore protects itself against any unexpected rise in the value of the currency.

Hedge Fund

An investment fund which deals in futures and options. These type of funds can be very risky.

Hire Purchase

Otherwise known as HP or buying on the never never. Hire Purchase agreements allow you to buy now and pay later. Because you will normally pay an interest rate on top of the purchase price, paying late will almost certainly mean paying more.

Hockey Stick

Used to describe the performance pattern, which when plotted on a graph, takes a long sliding decline and then starts to turn up again. The graph line looks like a hockey stick.

Holding Company

The head or parent company of a group which holds the shares of the other companies in the organisation.

is for instrument

IMAS

Integrated Monitoring and Surveillance System which is used by the London Stock Exchange authorities to identify unusual or unexplained share price movements. The system is a key part of its strategy to identify insider dealing.

Index-Linked

When the interest rate offered on any investment is linked to the official inflation rate.

Indication Only

A market-maker may offer an indication-only price for a share. This is exactly what it sounds like, it is an indication of the trading price but not a commitment to deal at that price.

Insider Dealing

The use of privileged or confidential information to make a profit on buying or selling shares. Insider dealing is a criminal offence. The Stock Exchange monitors all unusual price movements and carries out over 1,000 investigations into possible insider dealing each year. (See IMAS)

Instrument

A financial instrument is a catch all name for financial investment products, in other words things in which you can trade.

Interims

Companies generally report results twice a year. Once at the end of their financial year and once half-way through the year. The year end results are called finals and the other results are called interims. Interim results may be accompanied by an interim dividend.

Ere, don't they work in 'ospitals?

No, Lorraine, you're thinking of interns.

Am I? Oh. Well at least I know what IMAS means and I didn't even do Latin: IMO, IMAS, IMAT.

I think you're thinking of AMO, To Love, and it goes AMO, AMAS, AMAT... Close though.

Investment Banking

This is different from ordinary high street banks. Investment bankers drive fast cars, live in larger houses and eat in more expensive restaurants than their high street colleagues. The investment bank is concentrates on offering financial advice on investments, takeover deals, flotations and sell-offs.

Investment Clubs

It's tough out there in the cold world of the investor and to make it a little warmer some people club together to invest as part of a group instead of by themselves. Investment club members pay a subscription to join and the club then meets regularly to discuss which shares to buy with their subscription income. Investment clubs are useful ways of learning about shares and are often just excuses for friends to get together over a regular drink or meal. There is an introductory book to this area called 'Investment Clubs' by Tony Drury.

Investment Trust

A company which invests in shares. You can buy shares in investment trusts, so in effect you are buying a share of a group of shares. The investment trust therefore spreads your investment risk amongst many shares. (See unit trust)

is for junk bonds

Junk Bonds

Issued by companies with low credit ratings which offer the promise of high returns. Junk bonds have been most popular in the USA. The possibility of lots of profit means lots of risk as well.

Jobbers

Before the reforms of the Big Bang (see separate entry) there was a division between those who advised clients and those who dealt on their behalf. Jobbers bought and sold shares on the floor of the Stock Exchange but did not offer advice to clients. The advice bit was left to the brokers.

Kangaroo Bonds

Issued in Australian dollars in the US market.

Karat

A measure of the gold content so that one karat is equal to 1/24 pure gold and 24 karat gold is 100% pure gold.

Knife

Nickname for the New York Futures Exchange, taken from the sound of its initials (NYFE)

Kruggerand

A gold coin issued by South Africa.

Leveraged Buyout (LBO)

A takeover in which the buyer borrows money to purchase a controlling interest in a company.

LIBOR
The London Inter-Bank Offered Rate, otherwise known as the LIBOR, is the rate at which banks lend to one another.

Listing
When shares are traded officially on the stockmarket, they are said to have been given a listing and therefore appear on the stock exchange's daily Official List. They also appear on the list of quoted shares in the financial press.

Liquid
A term often used in reports on the financial markets. A liquid market is one where there are lots of buyers and seller. In such a situation trading is much easier than if there were few people willing to buy or sell stock.

Liquidate
To liquidate your investment is to turn it into cash by selling it.

Lobster Trap
A strategy to stop unwanted takeovers by focussing on the big shareholders. Real lobster traps do the same thing: catching the big lobsters and letting smaller fish go.

Lombard Rate
The name of the specific interest rate used in Germany. It is the rate at which the central bank lends to other commercial banks.

Long Bond
A bond that doesn't mature for at least 10 years.

Thought 'e said Long Blonde

LORRAINE'S ALTERNATIVE DEFINITIONS

LISTING: *What a ship does.*

LIQUIDATOR: *That's Arnold Schwarzenegger*

No. That's the Terminater your thinking of, not the Liquidator

is for movers & shakers

M & A

Short for Mergers and Acquisition – the process of companies either joining forces or one company taking control of another company.

Funny, I always get mixed up between M&S and S&M. The mind boggles at what M&A stands for.

Margin

a) The money you make above your cost is called the profit margin.
b) In the futures market you can buy a contract without handing over the full purchase price, all you need do is pay a percentage or margin of the full price. A margin call is therefore the time when you have to pay another slice of the purchase price.

Market Maker

A professional who buys and sells on his/her own account as opposed to doing it for someone else. A market maker is obliged to offer to buy and sell a specific set of securities. The presence of market makers ensures that the market remains operational and that trading can always take place as there is always someone willing to buy and sell shares. Market makers increase the liquidity of the market.

Maturity

When an investment reaches maturity it is time to cash it in, or in other words, have it redeemed.

MBI

Stands for Management Buy-In. An incoming management team (as opposed to one which was already there) which takes over not just the running but also ownership of the company. Also see MBO.

MBO

Stands for Management Buy-Out. The existing management team takes over the ownership of the company it already runs. MBO's became very popular in the 1980s.

Mergers

When two companies join forces without one partner having a particular dominance, as is the case in a takeover.

Mid Price

The price half way between the bid and offer prices. The mid prices are the ones quoted in the share price listings in the financial press. The mid price is a useful guide to the buying or selling price, but it is not the level at which the buying or selling actually takes place.

Movers & Shakers

The important people who act in the market with such force and power that they can move prices and shake things up.

is for nomad

Negotiable

Any instrument whose ownership can be transferred between different people is said to be negotiable. A bank note is transferable but an invitation to the Queen's garden party is not transferable, as it is meant only for the person to whom it was sent.

Everything is negotiable!

Net Asset Value

The value of a company after all its debts have been paid.

New Issue

A new issue of shares which brings a company to the stockmarket for the first time.

Nominal Value

The face value of a dividend coupon or other financial instrument.

NOMAD

Stands for Nominated Adviser. All AIM companies have a nominated adviser approved by the Stock Exchange.

Nominee

The name in which securities are registered and held in trust on behalf of the proper owner. A nominee account is therefore an account held on behalf of the proper owner. A broker often act as a nomines.

Non-voting shares

Although most shares allow the owner a right to have their say in the running of the business, proportional to the amount of shares they own, some shares carry no voting rights. In a flash of inspiration these shares were christened 'Non-voting shares'.

NYSE

Stands for New York Stock Exchange, the main exchange in the USA. Also known as the Big Board.

is for old lady

Offer Price
The price at which shares are offered to investors.

Ofex
The third exchange in London after the official Stock Exchange and the Alternative Investment Market. The market is run by J.P. Jenkins.

Old Lady of Threadneedle Street
Nickname for the Bank of England.

Open Outcry
When buying and selling takes place with traders shouting and signalling their bids and offers across a trading floor. Since the changes brought about by Big Bang, shares are no longer traded in this way and are bought and sold via computer. Futures and options are still traded by an open outcry system.

Operating Profit
The profit made by a company from selling its products or services. Other factors also have an effect on the overall profitability of the company, including interest charges on

overdrafts, depreciation of capital, and unusual one-off costs. The pretax profit figure, before and after exceptional costs, is the one most often used to represent the overall performance of the company.

Options

A contract which gives the holder the right but not the obligation to buy or sell a quantity of any particular product, at a specific price and time in the future. Option are a form of derivative.

Ordinary Shares

Owners of ordinary shares are entitled to part of the dividend payments which are made. They also become part owners of the company and the more shares they have, the larger the proportion of the company they own. Ordinary share owners have voting rights and therefore can help determine the future direction of the company.

Out of Money

A call option is out of money when the price of the option can be exercised at is higher than the market price.

LORRAINE'S ALTERNATIVE DEFINITIONS

OPTIONS: Mmmm.... Chocolate drink

is for puppy

Partly Paid

Shares are sometimes issued on a partly paid basis, which means that the owners of the shares have to pay for them in a number of installments.

PEP

Otherwise known as Personal Equity Plan. PEPs were launched in the 1980s as a way of encouraging people to invest in shares by offering investors tax incentives.

P/E Ratio

Otherwise known as price/earnings ratio. It is used to help determine whether a share is cheap or expensive in terms of the earnings of the underlying business.

PIA

Personal Investment Authority is the main retail financial regulator and therefore the one you're most likely to come in contact with.

Pit

On the floor of LIFFE (London International Financial Futures and Options Exchange) trading is divided into various different areas in which different products are traded. Each area is called a trading pit. The mad shouting and shoving makes the place look like a fighting pit, so the name is very relevant.

Placing

A private sale of shares which can be used by large sellers of shares to dispose of the equity in one pre-arranged deal. Rules governing placings are issued by the London Stock Exchange.

Plc

Often seen after the name of a company, the initials stand for public limited company.

Preference Share

These offer a fixed dividend each year and do not usually come with voting rights. In the great scheme of things preference share holders rank ahead of ordinary shareholders, but behind debenture holders, in their claims on the company.

Privatisation
The process by which a state owned company transfers to private ownership through the issue and sale of shares.

Programme Trading
A computer-run trading system which issues buy or sell orders once the market drops below or above key support levels. Because programme trading can result in massive quantities of shares being traded, the system can exaggerate the size of any fall or rise in the general value of share prices. It has therefore been blamed for increasing the volatility of the market.

Proxy Vote
A vote taken on behalf of a shareholder because he/she cannot attend the meeting at which the vote will take place.

Put
An option to sell shares, commodities and bonds. A put option is a form of derivative.

Puppy
Remember the YUPPY (Young Urban Professionals), the type of power dressed, mobile phone totting, fast car driving, champagne swilling creatures of the 80's? Well many of them have moved out to the quieter life of the suburbs and become PUPPIES – Previously Young Urban Professionals.

LORRAINE'S ALTERNATIVE DEFINITIONS

P/E RATIO: Changing room pong X Coldness of showers = Number of letters excusing you from gym

PUT: What they do in golf

Q

is for the quiet life

Q

Qualifies as the quintessential quandary for glossary compilers, since there is not only a low quantity but also a low quality of q's to talk about. What we need is a quantum leap in the amount of Q's in the financial lexicon. In short there are no Q's of which to talk – so Q is for the quiet life.

Well you've only forgotten the most important word of all – quid or pound, the getting of which is what this whole book is about.

is for rio trading

Rate of Return
The rate at which your investment increases in value.

Receiver
A receiver is appointed to recover debts from a company. The appointment of a receiver usually leads to the eventual closure of the company.

Redemption Date
The date on which a security is due to be repaid.

Registrar
The days of shouting 'Yes miss' are not over, even if you are out of shorts and haven't done your homework for over 20 years. Once you're a shareholder, you're back in the classroom having to take the register. Each public company must maintain a list of its shareholders so it knows who owns the company, who it must contact in case votes need to be taken on the company's future and who to send the dividend cheques to. The person or organisation which takes responsibility for looking after and maintaining the company's register is the Registrar.

Rights Issue

A rights issue is a way for a public company to raise more finance through the issue of new shares. The rights issue invites existing shareholders to buy more shares in the company. Shareholders are allowed to buy in proportion to the amount they already own. So a person who owns 100 shares in the company will be allowed to buy more new shares than a person who owns just 10.

Rio Trading

This is when a trader takes an exceptionally risky position in the markets ahead of a major price sensitive announcement and then books a flight to Rio De Janiero. Just before the flight leaves, the trader calls the office to find out whether the gamble was successful. If it was a success, the trader returns to the office as a conquering hero, to the sound of applause and the thump of his big bonus. If the bet was unsuccessful, the trader boards the plane and spends the next few years getting a sun tan and writing a novel.

Robinson Crusoe Week

A week in which a major announcement is expected on Friday so investors sit on their hands doing nothing until they hear the news. They are therefore waiting for Friday just as Robinson Crusoe did on his desert island.

Ahhh no. It was definitely longer than a week. Five weeks in Bournemouth with Tessa Sanderson playing my Man Friday. Oooh and there was that drop dead gorgeous gladiator. The big one. The really big huge one – oh yes... Trojan.

Rolling Settlement

The name of the system in which share purchases must be paid for within a certain number of days following the transaction.

is for stags

Samurai
A Japanese bond held by a non-resident.

Scrip Issue
Otherwise known as a capitalisation or bonus issue. Scrip issues take place when a company distributes new shares to its existing shareholder base but does not charge them for the shares. After a scrip issue, the price of individual shares will usually fall, although because shareholders will now have more shares, the actual total value of their holdings is likely to to remain the same. The amount of new shares anyone receives is calculated on the amount they already own. Scrip issues are made when a company feels the price of each share has got too high and it would be useful or beneficial to reduce the unit price of each share.

Securities
General name for stocks and shares.

Short
Going short means selling something you don't own in the hope that you can buy it back at a cheaper price, before you have to deliver the product to your customer. Also used to describe a government bond which has less than five years to mature. (Also see Long)

SIB
The Securities and Investments Board is responsible for regulating the whole investment industry and is therefore the most senior regulating body in the City

Spot

When you deal in the spot market, you are buying or selling for immediate delivery.

Spread

The difference between the bid and offer price. The spread is where the market maker finds the profit on each trade.

Stags

"The world is full of beautiful things, buttercup wings, fairy tale things" as Dr. Doolittle said, and in the 80s it became filled with stags as well. These are the people who hope they can make a profit by buying into a new issue of shares and then selling as soon as dealing begins. Many of the large privatisations encouraged the stags, as it was widely thought that a quick profit could be made.

Stalking Horse

In corporate takeovers a stalking horse may start the process of bidding for a company only to be overtaken by some stronger predator who reveals himself at the last minute.

Stamp Duty

The tax payable on all purchases of shares.

Sterling

Another word for the pound in your pocket (or overdraft).

Stockbroker

A person or company which buys and sells shares on behalf of its clients.

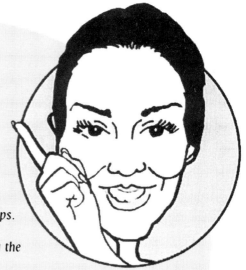

LORRAINE'S ALTERNATIVE DEFINITIONS

SHORT: *What you are Adam.*

SPOT: *The dog out of the Wooden Tops.*

SUPPORT LEVELS: *Way of assessing the elastic content of a corset.*

SUSPENSION: *What I'm kept in most of the time.*

I think you mean suspense

Stop-loss

A stop-loss investment system is one in which you sell once any investment has lost a certain amount of its value. Although it may be difficult to convince oneself to sell a share if you think it may go up in value later on, Stop-loss strategies at least limit the level of loss you can suffer.

Stop-loss insurance policies are also issued by the insurance market, Lloyds of London. The policies insure the market's investors, known as names, against any losses they may make. The extent of the protection offered by these policies varies according to the cover which is required by the individual name.

Support Levels

In many of the newspaper stockmarket or currency reports, you will read about investments hitting key support levels. Think of these as important milestones along the price graph of any currency, commodity or equity. If any of these investments drops below a key support level the market may become scared that it won't find more support until it reaches a much lower level. In such circumstances the investment appears even less attractive and can come under further heavy selling pressure.

Suspension

A share may be suspended from the stockmarket if a takeover bid is underway or to enable the publication of the full details of any move it is planning. The share suspension therefore acts to reduce ill-informed or rumour-driven trading.

Swaps

There are two main types of interest rate swaps:

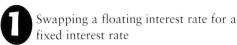 Swapping a floating interest rate for a fixed interest rate

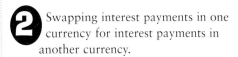 Swapping interest payments in one currency for interest payments in another currency.

is for triple witching

Target

A company which is about to be taken over is called the target.

Technical Analysis

The method of predicting future price movements by studying the past patterns of price movements. Because this involves spending hours hunched over graphs and charts, practitioners of this particular art are called Chartists. (See fundamental analysis)

Tender Offer

A type of auction in which would be buyers say how much they are willing to offer for shares or bonds, which are then sold to the highest bidders.

Tick

The smallest price movement recognised on any particular financial exchange. The size of a tick changes according to which investment you are talking about.

Touch

The best buying and selling prices offered by the various market makers in the City. If you want to buy some Marks and Spencers shares, market makers may offer a range of different prices: some may sell at 478 other at 476 and some may buy at 479 or 478. The touch is the best selling and buying prices which in the above example would be 476-479 and your broker would look for the touch in carrying out your trading order.

Triple Witching Hour
The final hour before the expiry of equity, index options and index futures contracts. It usually brings some heavy trading on the markets.

Unbundling
Breaking up a company into its constituent parts. The idea is that a company may be worth more when sold as individual parts than when it's sold as a whole.

Underwrite
Bringing any new company to the stockmarket always involves some risk, not least that no one may want to buy the shares you're so kindly offering them. To reduce this risk, a new company can ask for the share issue to be underwritten. The underwriter guarantees that they will buy any of the shares not sold on the stockmarket. The company must pay the underwriter a fee for this service.

Unit Trusts
A means of spreading your risk amongst a number of different investments. Unit trusts are similar to investment trusts but if you buy a unit of a unit trust, its price directly reflects the value of the underlying investments. investment trusts are quoted on the stockmarket and their shares do not completely reflect the value of the investments. See the Product Pack for more details.

is for venture capitalist

Vendor
The seller.

Venture Capitalist
Venture capitalists provide funding for the setting-up or expansion of businesses. They fill a much needed gap which lies between the finance offered by bank overdrafts and loans and the funding available through a stockmarket flotation.

Wall Street
The location of the New York Stock Exchange and often used to refer to the exchange itself.

Warrant
An option to buy a company's shares – which if you've been paying attention may sound exactly like a call option. Warrants are different from call options in that they cover longer periods, usually three to ten years.

White Knight
A company which saves another company from an unwelcome takeover bid by taking over the company itself. The target company still finds itself with a new master but one it finds more palatable than the original bidder.

Yield
The annual income from an investment calculated as a percentage of its market price.

Index

Black Economy 116

black knight term 116

Black Monday 116

Blue Chip companies 116

bonds 116

    convertible 56, 59

    corporate 54-9

    gilts, risks comparison 55, 59

    government 54-9

    interest rates 57

    investment 10, 11, 13

    price fluctuation 54

    transferring ownership 54

bottom feeding 116

break even point term 116

brokers 35-9, 117

    charges 36

    directory 37-8

    fees 17

    hand signals 72

    services offered 35-6, 86-8

building societies

    conversion to banks 17

    investment 10, 11, 13

    yield figures 12

Building Society Association 78

Building Society Investor Protection Scheme 78-9

bull markets 25, 117

business plans 117

C

Call Options 69, 118

Capital Bonds, National Savings 101

capital gains tax 41-2, 55

capital shares 50

cash cow 118

cash market term 118

Catholic Building Society 63

Central Register 76-7

chartists 118

Childrens Bonus Bonds 102

Chinese Walls 118

chocolate cheesecake recipe 23

Co-operative Bank, investment 61

Coats Viyella, shareholder benefits 29

commission 26, 39, 118

commodities 10, 11, 119

commodity and energy trust 51

companies

    see also investment; shares

    NAV 21

company bonds 13

compensation 77

consumers, power of 64

Convertible Bonds 56, 59

convertibles trust 52

Corporate Bonds 54-9, 95

    PEPs 43

    risks 95

    suitability 95

country trust 52

coupon rate, bonds 56

coupons 119

Cum dividend 119

currency futures, derivatives 70

currency holdings, investment 10, 11

current accounts, falling value 10

Cyclical stock 119

D

dawn raid 120

'dead cat bounce' 120

deal on the margin 67

dealer term 120

debentures 55, 120

Deposit Protection Scheme 78-9

depreciation 120

derivatives 65-73

    history 66

    investment 10, 11, 13

    warrants 50

directors, share dealings tip 36

discounts, shares 27

discretionary service, brokers 35-6

dividends 10, 12, 18, 20, 120

    yield calculation 21

Dow Jones Industrial Index 121

downgrade term 121

downsizing 121

E

earnings multiple 33

earnings per share 122

Ecology Building Society 62

ECU *see* European Currency Unit

EGM *see* Extraordinary General Meeting

EIRIS *see* Ethical Investment Research Institute

Electronic Random Number Indicator

    Equipment 107

endowment mortgages 122-3

entrepreneur term 123

equities 123

    yield figures 12

ERM *see* Exchange Rate Mechanism

ERNIE *see* Electronic Random Number

    Indicator Equipment

Ethical Investment Research Institute (EIRIS)

    61, 64

ethical investments 60-4

    advisers 61, 64

    definition 60

    Triodos Bank 62

Eurobonds 123

European Currency Unit (ECU) 122

ex term 123

exchange rate 123

Exchange Rate Mechanism (ERM) 123

execution only service 123

execution service, brokers 35, 39

expiry term 123

Extraordinary General Meeting (EGM) 122

F

Federal Reserve 124

final dividend term 124

financial advisors 74-5, 124

financial analysts 118

financial instruments 129

financial and property trust 51

Financial Times (FT) 34

First Option Bonds, National Savings 99

fiscal year 124

fixed rate 124

flipper term 125

floating rate 124

flotation 124

fraud

    Central Register 76

    compensation 77

FT Stock Exchange Futures 69

FT Stock Exchange Index (FTSE) 125

    All Share Index 48

FTSE *see* FT Stock Exchange Index

fund of funds trust 52

fundamental analysis 125

futures 40

    contracts 65, 69

    currency 70

    options 96

futures market 125

G

gearing 126

GEMMs *see* gilt-edged market makers

General Accident, shareholder benefits 29

gilt-edged market makers (GEMMs) 126

gilts (gilt edged stocks) 13, 42, 54-9, 94, 126

    bonds comparison 55

    government stock 94

    interest rates 56-9

    long 55

    medium 55

Goodbye, it's been nice having you